ENGLISH RECUSANT LITERATURE
1558–1640

Selected and Edited by
D. M. ROGERS

Volume 294

ST. GREGORY
The Second Booke of the Dialogues
1638

ST. GREGORY
The Second Booke of the Dialogues
1638

The Scolar Press
1976

ISBN o 85967 295 6

Published and printed in Great Britain by
The Scolar Press Limited, 59-61 East Parade,
Ilkley, Yorkshire and
39 Great Russell Street,
London WC1

NOTE

Reproduced (original size) from a copy in the library of the Brompton Oratory, by permission of the Provost and Fathers. In this copy the *Short treatise touching the confraternitie of the scapular of St. Benedicts order* (1639) is bound before the *Second booke*; in the facsimile the *Short treatise* follows the second part, *The rule*.

References: Allison and Rogers 369; STC 12350 and [1020].

THE SECOND BOOKE
OF THE DIALOGVES
OF
S. GREGORIE
THE GREATE, THE FIRST
POPE OF THAT NAME
CONTAININGE THE LIFE
AND MIRACLES OF
OVR HOLIE FATHER
S. BENEDICT.

*To which is adioined the Rule of
the same* HOLIE PATRIARCHE
*translated into the Englishe
tonge by* C. F. *priest
& Monke of the
same order.*

Permissu superiorum
Printed Ann. 1638.

TO THE HONORABLE
MISTRESSE

Mrs ANNE CARIE

DAVGHTER TO THE

LORD VICOVNT

OF FAVKLAND.

 ISTRESSE CARIE,

Since my first zeale of printinge this worke I haue had
two notable obiections: the first
because I could not vse means
more effectuall to discouer my
owne vnworthines: the other

A 2   (if

THE EPISTLE

(if in the Epiſtle Dedicato-
rie which was left to mee) I
should ſpeake of your worth
and vertue, accordinge to my
owne conscience, to them whoe
know you not I should be
thought extreamlie to flatter; to
that them that know you malitious or ignorant. Theſe are
the reaſons which ſtaied the
printinge of it , & cauſed mée
to ſeeke to ingage ſome in the
makinge of an Epiſtle, whoe by
reaſon of theare neerenes to you,
might ſeeme to ſome to be excluded from it, but to mee moſt fitt,
thinkinge noe other worthie to
commende yow. Hee that tranſ-
lated

lated part of it (whoe *I am sure*
hath a prime place in your me-
morie) intended it to you, but since
death preuented him from doinge
this (though *I* hope it hath ina-
bleied him to doe you better seruice by prayinge for you & all
your familie in heauen) *I* haue
taken vpon mee to supplie his
place in finishinge & dedica-
tinge this to you. Our holie Father *S. Benedict* whose *Rule*
in our time hath neuer bene
wholie translated in to the
English tonge, deserues a re-
uerent respect from all the world,
but especially from *English*
men, since his children cannot

THE EPISTLE

be denied the honor of conuer-
tinge this country to the faith of
Christ. And for this present of
S. Benedicts to my country, part
of the obligation is due to you
for whom it was principallie
done. God blesse you with perse-
uerāce in those giftes hee hath be-
stowed vpon you, and to that end
hee shall be often solicited by.

Your deuoted beadsman.
B. E. T.

THE SECOND BOOKE
OF THE DIALOGVES
OF
S. GREGORIE
THE GREATE,
CONTAINING THE LIFE
AND MIRACLES
OF S. BENEDICT.

ENEDICT bleſſed by
name and grace was à
man of venerable life,
from his very child hood
graue and ſtayed for his
demeanonr ſurpaſſing his age, he gaue
himſelfe to no diſport or pleaſure; but

A 4   liuing

liuing heere vpon earth , he despised
the world with all the glory thereof at
such time as he might haue most
freely enioyed it. He was borne in the
prouince of Nursia , and from thence
sent to Rome to study the liberall
sciences. But when he saw there many
through the vneeuen pathes of vice
runne headlong to their owne ruine,
he drew back his foot , but new set in
to the world, least in the search of hu-
maine knowledge , he might also fall
in to the same dangerous precipice :
Thus cotemning learning and studies,
& abandonning his fathers howse and
goods, he desired onely to please god
in à vertuous life. So that he departed
skilfully ignorant , and wisely vnlear-
ned. I haue not attained vnto all this
man did, but these few things wich I
heere set downe were related vnto
me by fower of his disciples , namely
Constantine à very Reuerend man
who succeded him in the gouernment
of the Monastery in monte Cassino.
Valentiniane who for many yeares bare
                                    Rule

Rule in the Monaſtery of Lateran. Simplicius likewiſe who was third ſuperiour of that Conuent after him, & Honoratus who yet gouerneth the Monaſtery which he firſt inhabited.

How St. Benedict miraculouſly
made whole a brooken
ſieue.

CHAP. I.

BEnedict hauing now left the ſchooles reſolued forth with to bee take himſelfe to the deſert, accompanied onely with his nurſe who moſt tenderly loued him, and would by no meanes part from him. Comming therefore to à place called Suſide, and remaining for ſome time in the church of S. Peter by the charitable inuitement of many vertuous people who liued there for deuotion; So it chanced that his nurſe borroed of a neighbour a ſieue to cleanſe wheate, which being left careleſly vpon the table was found

A 5 broken

brokē in two peeces. Wherefore at her
retourne finding it broke, she began to
weepe bitterly becaufe it was onely
lent her. But Religious and pious Benedict, feeing his Nurfe to lament in that
manner was mooued with compaffion,
and taking with him the two peeces
of the broken fieue, with teares he feil
to his prayers, which no fooner ended,
but he found the fieue whole and found
not any figne remaining that it had
beene broken. Thē prefently retourning to his nurfe he reftored to her the
fieue whole to her exceeding comfort.
This miracle was diuulged vnto all
that liued thereabout, and fo much ad-
mired by all, that the in habitans of that
place caufed the fame to be hanged vp
in the church porch, that not onely
thofe who were then liuing, but all po-
fterity might know with how great
giftes of grace Benedict was endoued
from the begining of his conuerfion.
The fieue remained to be feene for
many yeares after, and hung ouer the
church doore euen vntill the troubles

of

of the Longobardes. But Benedict
more defirous to fuffer croffes and af-
flictions in this world, then couetous
of praife, and rather willing to vndergoe labours for the honoure of
God, then to be extolled with the fa-
uors of this world, fled fecretly from
his nurfe to à remote place in the defert
called Sublacus, diftant forty miles from
Rome, in which à fountaine fpringing
with coole, and chriftall waters, ex-
tendeth it felfe at firft in to à broade
lake, and running farther with en-
creafe of waters, be cometh at the laft
à riuer. As he was trauelling to the
place, à certaine Monke called Roma
nus mett him, and asked whither he
was going, hauing vnderftood his intention, he both kept it fecrett, and
affoarded him his beft helpe, moreouer
he gaue him a Religious habitt and
affifted him in all things. The man of
God being come to this place, liued for
the fpace of three yeares in an obfcure
caue vnknowne to any man except
Romanus the Monke, who liued not
far of

far of in a Monaſtery gouerned by fa:
Theodacus, from whence he would
piouſly ſteale forth, and vpon certaine
dayes bring to Benedict a loafe of bread
which he had ſpared from his owne allowance. But there being no way to
the caue from Romanus his cell by
reaſon of a ſteepe and hige rock which
hung ouer it, Romanus vſed to lett
downe the loafe by a long corde to
which alſo he faſtened a litle bell, that
by the ſound of it the man of God
might know when Romanus brought
him the bread. But the old enimie en-
uying the charity of the one, and the
refection of the other, when on à certaine day he beheld the bread lett
downe in this manner, threw a ſtone
and brake it. Not withſtanding Romanus afterward failed not to aſſiſt him
in the beſt manner he was able. Now
when it pleaſed the diuine goodnes to
free Romanus from his labours, and
manifeſt to the world the life of St. Benedict for an example to all men, that
the candle ſet vpon à candleſtick might
                                    ſhine,

shine, and giue light to the whole church of God, our Lord vouchsafed to appeare to à certaine priest liuing far of, who had made ready his dinner for easter day, saying to him, thou hast prepared good cheare for thy selfe, and my seruant in such à place is famished for hunger, who presently rose vp, and on the solemne day of Easter went towards the place with such meate as he had prouided for himselfe, where seeking the man of God amongst craggie rockes, winding vallies and hollow pits, he found him hidde in à caue. Then after prayers, and thankes giuing to God they sat downe, and after some spirituall discourse the Priest said. Rise Brother and let vs take our refection, for this is Easter day. To whom the man of God answered, I know it is Easter with me, because I haue found so much fauour in the sight of God, as this day to enioy your company. (For not hauing à long time conuersed with men, he did not know it was Easter day.) The good Priest did therefore a-

gaine

gaine affirme it, saying trulie this is the
day of our Lords Resurrection, and
therefore it is not fitt you should keepe
abstinence, and for this cause I am sent
that wee may eate together, that which
Allmighty God hath pleased to bestow
vpon vs. Where vpon they said grace,
and fell to their meate; their discourse
and dinner ended the priest retourned
to his church. About the same time
certaine shepheards found him hid in
à caue, who at the first espieing him
amongst the bushes cloathed in the
skinnes of beasts, tooke him for some
wilde beast ; but afterwards knowing
him to be à man of God, many of them
were conuerted from their sauadge life
to vertue. By this meanes his name beganne to be famous in the country; and
many did resort vnto him bringing
with them necessaries for his corporall
nourishment, for which they receiued
spirituall foode.

*How he ouercam à grieuous tentation
of the flesh.*

Chap. II.

THe Holy man being on à certaine
day alone, the temptour was at
hand, & in the likeness of à litle black
bird commonly called an owzell began
to flie about his face, and that so neare,
and so often as he might haue taken
her with his hand; But no sooner had
he blessed himselfe with the signe of
the crosse, but it vanished. When presently so great à carnall tentation as-
sailed him, that in his life he neuer had
felt the like. For the remembrance of
à woman which sometime he had
seene was so liuely represented to his
fancy by the wicked spiritt, and so ve-
hemently did her image inflame his
breast with lustfull desires, that almost
ouercome with pleasure, he was determining to leaue the wildernes. But sud-
dainly assisted with diuine grace, he
came

came to himselfe, and seing neare him
à thicket full of nettles and bryars, he
threw of his garments, and cast himselfe naked in to the middest of them,
there wallowing and rooling himselfe
in those sharpe thornes and nettels; so
that when he rose vp, his body was all
pittifully rent and torne. Thus by the
wounds of his flesh, he cured those of
his soule by tourning pleasure in to
paine, and by the vehemence of out-
ward torments, he extinguished the
vnlawfull flame which burnt within
him, ouer coming sinne by changing
the fire. After which time as he himselfe related to his disciples, he was so
free from the like temptation, that he
neuer felt any such motion. Many after this beganne to forsake the world,
and put themselues vnder his gouernment; for being now altogether free
from vice, he worthily deserued to be
made a Maister of vertue. As in Exo-
dus God commanded by Moyses, that
the Leuites should from fiue and
twenty yeares and vpward, and after
fifty

fifty yeares they should be appointed to keepe the holy vehels.

Peter.

I Haue already vnderstood something of this testimony alleadged, yet I pray make it more plaine vnto me.

Gregory.

IT is manifest Peter that in youth the tentations of the flesh are greate, but after fifty naturall heate waxeth colde; Now the soules of good men are the holy vessels, and therefore while the elect are in tentation it is necessary that they liue vnder obedience, and be wearied with labours, but when by reason of their age the feruor of temptation is aswaged, they are ordained keepers of holy vessels, that is become instructours of soules.

Pe-

Peter.

I Confesse you haue giuen me full satisfaction, and therefore this place of scripture being clearely expounded I pray goe on with the holy mans life.

How St. Benedict brake à glasse in peeces by making the signe of the holy crosse.

CHAP. III.

HAuing thus vanquished this tentation, the man of God like à good soile well manured and weeded, brought forth aboundant fruite of the seede of vertue. So that the fame of his sanctity beganne to spread it selfe more largely. Not far of was à Monastery whose Abbot being dead the whole Conuent repaired to the venerable man Benedict, and with earnest perswasions requested him for

their

their Abbot, which he refuſed for à
longe time, forewarning them that his
manner of life and theirs were not a-
greable; yet at length ouer come with
importunity he gaue his conſent. But
when in the ſame Monaſtery he beganne to obſerue Regular diſcipline, ſo
that none of the Monkes (as in former
time) were permitted by their diſor-
der to ſwerue any way from the path
of vertue, they repented themſelues of
their choiſe in receiuing him for their
Superiour, whoſe integrity of life was
diſproportionable to their peruerſenes.
And therefore when they perceiued
themſelues reſtrained from vnlawfull
acts, it greiued them to leaue their deſires, and hard it was to relinquiſh old
cuſtomes, and beginne a new life: be-
ſide the conuerſation of good men is
alwayes odious to the wicked, they
begane therefore to plot his death, &
after conſultation had together, they
poiſened his wine. So when the glaſſe
which cōtained the empoiſened drinke
was according to the cuſtome of the
Mo-

Monaſtery preſented at table to be
bleſſed by the Abbot, Benedict putting
forth his hande and maknig the ſigne
of the croſſ, the glaſſe which was held
far of preſently brake in peeces, as if
in ſtead of bleſſing it, he had throwne
à ſtone againſt it. By this the man of
God perceaued eaſely that the glaſſ had
in it, the drinke of death which could
not indure the ſigne of life. So preſently
riſing vp with a mild and cheerefull
countenance, hauing called the Brethren together, he thus ſpake vnto thē.
Almighty God of his mercy forgiue
you Brethren, why haue you dealt
thus with me? Did not I fortell you
that my māner of life and yours would
not agree: Goe and ſeeke à Superiour
to your liking, for you can haue me no
longer with you. This ſaid he forth
with retourned to the ſolitude he loued
ſo well, and liued there with himſelfe
in the ſight of him who ſeeth all
things.

Peter.

Peter.

I Doe not well vnderstand what
you meane he liued with him
selfe.

Gregory.

IF the Holy man had bin longer
constrained to gouerne those mōkes
who had all conspired against him, and
were so contrary to him in life and
manners, it might peraduenture haue
diminished his owne vigour and feruour of deuotion, with drawing his
mind from the light of contemplation,
so that ouer much busied in correcting
the faults of others, he might haue
neglected his owne; and so perhaps
lost himselfe & yet not gained others.
For as often as by contagious motions
wee are transported out of our selfes,
we remaine the same, but not with ourselfes, because not looking in to our
owne actions, wee are vandring a-
bout

bout others things; for doe we thinke
that he was with himselfe who went
in to à far countrie, consumed the portion allotted to him, and after he had
put himselfe in to the seruice of à citi-
zen of that country, kept his hogges
and was glad to fill his belly with the
huskes they eate; not with standing
when he began to consider what he
had lost (as the scripture testifieth)
being come to himselfe he said. How
many of my fathers hirelings haue plenty of bread? For if he were before with
himselfe, how was it true that he retourned to himselfe? I may well say
therefore that this holy man liued with
himselfe, because he neuer turned the
eye of his soule from himselfe, but standing alwayes on his guard with great
circumspection he kept himselfe continually in the sight of the all seeing
eye of his Creatour.

Peter.

HOw is it then to be vnderstood
which is written of St. Peter the
A-

Apostle, when he was led by the Angell out of the prison? Who retourning to himselfe said, now I know assuredly that our Lord hath sent his Angell, & hath deliuered me out of the handes of Herod, and from all he expectation of the people of the Iewes.

Gregory.

TWo wayes Peter we are caryed out ef our selues: for either by lubricity of thought wee fall beneath ourselfes; or by the grace of contemplation we are raysed aboue our selfes. He therefore that kept the hogges by his inconstancy of minde and vncleanesse, fell beneath himselfe; but he whom the Angell loosed, and rauished in to an extasie, was indeed also out of himselfe, but yet aboue himselfe. But both of them retourned to the selfes, the one when reclaming his lewd life he was conuerted at heart, the other when from the height of contemplation he retourned to his na-
                                    turall

turall and ordinary vnderſtanding.
Thus venerable Benedict in that ſolitude dwelt with himſelfe for as much as
he kept himſelfe with in his thoughts;
for as often as by the feruour of contemplation he was eleuated, with out
doubt he left himſelfe as it were beneath himſelfe.

Peter.

I Like well this you ſay, but re-
ſolue me, I pray you, should he
haue left thoſe Monkes of whom he
had once taken charge.

Gregory.

IN my opinion Peter, a bad cõmu-
nity may be tollerated where there
are found at leaſt ſome good which
ma y be helped, but where there is no
benefitt to be expected of any good,
labour is many times loſt vpon the bad:
eſpecially if there be any other preſent
occaſions whereni we may do God
better

better feruice. Now who was there
whom the holy man should haue ſtaied
to gouerne, when they had all conſpi-
red againſt him. And many things are
confidered by the perfect which ought
not to be paſſed in ſilence; for they perceiuing their endeauors to be without
effect; depart to ſome other place there
to employ themſelues more profitablely.
Wherefore that famous Preacher who
defireth to be diſſolued and be with
Chriſt, vnto whom to liue is Chriſt
and to dye is gayne, did not onely defire himſelfe to ſuffer, but did alſo ani-
mate and encourage others to vndergoe the like. He I ſay, being per-
ſecuted at Damaſcus cauſed himſelfe
to be let downe from the wall by a
cord and basket, whereby he eſcaped
priuately. Shall we ſay then that Paul
feared death which he earneſtly defired
for the loue of Chriſt as appeareth by
his owne teſtimony. No ſurely, but
whereas he fore ſaw that his endeauors there would profitt litle, with
much hazard and difficulty he reſerued

B   himſelfe

himſelfe to labour in an other place with better ſucceſſe. For this valiant champion of Allmighty God would not be confined to ſo narrow limitts, but enlarged himſelfe to ſeeke battels in the open field. So you may obſerue that the holy man Benedict lefte not ſo many incorrigibile in that place, as he conuerted to à ſpirituall life els where.

Peter.

YOu ſay true as both reaſon and the example alleadged prooues, but I pray, retourne to proſecute the life of this holy Father.

Gregory.

THe Holy man for many yeares encreaſed wonderfully in vertues and Miracles, whereby a great number in thoſe parts were gathered together in the ſeruice of God; So that by the aſſiſtance of our Lord Ieſus he built there

there twelue Monasteries , in each of
which he put twelue Monkes with
their Superiours ; and retained a few
with himselfe whom he thought to
instruct further. Now began diuers
Noble and deuout personages from
Rome to resort to him; and commended their children to be brought vp by
him in the seruice of God. At the same
time Eunicius brought vnto him Maurus, and Tertullius à Senatour his sonne
Placidus both very hopefull children , of which two , Maurus although young yet by reason of his fore-
wardenes in the schoole of vertue,
began to assist his Maister; but Placidus was as yet à child of tender
yeares.

How he reclamed An indeuout
Monke.

Chap. IV.

IN one of those Monasteries which
the holy man had built there about

was à certaine Monke that could not
stay at his prayers, but so soone as he
saw his brethren knele and dispose
themselues for their mentall prayer,
he would goe out, and there spend his
wandering thoughts vpon wordly and
transitory things. For which hauing
bin often admonished by his Abbot, he
was brought before the man of God,
who also sharpely reprehended him for
his folly; but retourning to his Monastery he scarce remembred two dayes
what had bin said vnto him, for the
third day he fell to his old custome, and
at the time of prayer went out againe,
where of when the holy man was informed by the Abbot the second time,
he said, I will come my selfe and re-
forme him. And when he was come
to the same Monastery, and the Brethren after the Psalmes ended at the
accoustomed time betooke themselfes
to prayer; He perceued à litle black
boy who pulled this Monke out by
the hemme of his garment, which he
insinuated secretly to Pompeianus Abbot

bot of the Monaſtery, and to Maurus
ſaying, ſee you not there who it is that
draweth this Monke out? who anſwered noe. Let vs pray (replyed he') that
you may likewiſe ſee whom this
Monke followeth. After prayer continued for two dayes Maurus ſaw; but
Pompeianus cold not perceiue any
thing. The next day when the man
of God had finiſhed his prayer, he went
out of the oratory and found the
Monke ſtanding with out, whom he
forth with ſtrake with à wane for his
obſtinacy and boulddenes of heart, and
from that time euer after the Monke
was free from the wicked ſuggeſtion
of the black boy, and remained con-
ſtant at his prayers. For the wicked
fiend as if himſelfe had bin beaten, durſt
no more tempt him to the like offence.

How by the prayers of St. Benedict A
spring issued from the topo of
a mountaine.

CHAP. V.

THree of the Monasteries which
he foūded in that place, were built
vpon the cliffes of à mountaine, which
was very troublesome to the Monkes
to be forced to fetch vp their water fiō
the lake, for besides the toyle, it was
also dangerous by reason of the high
and steepie descent. Heere vpon the
Religious of these three Monasteries
came all together to the seruant of God
Benedict ; and told him it was very
troublesome to goe downe for water
as far as the lake , and therefore the
Monasteries of necessity , were to be
remooued to some more commodious
place. The holy man with confortable
words dismissed them , and at night
with litle Placidus (whom we mentioned

tioned before) went vp to the rock, and
there prayed à long time, and hauing
ended his prayers, he putt three stones
for à marke in the same place; and so
vnknowne to all, he retourned to his
Monastery. Not long after when the
Brethren came againe to him for want
of water, goe (saith he) and on the
rock where you shall finde three
stones one vpon an other digge à litle,
for Allmighty God is able to make water spring from the top of that mountaine, that you may be eased of this labour. At their retourne to the mountaine they found already the signes of
water in the rock, as Benedict fore told
them, so à pitt being digged, it was presently full with water which issueth
forth so plentifully, that to this day it
continueth running downe to the foot
of the mountaine.

How

*How he miraculously caused the iron
head of à bile fallen in to the water,
to fasten it selfe againe in
the haft.*

CHAP. VI.

A Certaine poore Goth desirous
to lead à Religious life, repaired
to the man of God Benedict, who most
willngly receiued him; and one day
willed the Brethren to giue him à bile
to cutt vp brambles in à place which
he intended for à garden. This place
which the Goth had vndertaken to ac-
comodate, was ouer the lakes side.
Whilest the Goth laboured à maine in
cutting vp the thicke bryars, the iron
slipping out of the handle, fell into the
lake in à place so deepe, that there was
no hope to recouer it. The Goth hauing
lost his bile was in great perplexity
rune to the Monke Maurus, and told
him the mischance, who presently ad-
uertised Benedict thereof, and immediately

diately the holy man came himselfe to the lake , tooke the haft out of the Goths hand,and caſt it in to the water, when behold,the iron roſe vp from the bottome and entered in to the haft as before , which he there rendered to the Goth ſaying , take it and worke on cheerefully and be not diſcomforted.

How Maurus walked vpon the water.

CHAP. VII.

ONe day as venerable Benedict was in his cell,yong Placidus (à Monke of his) went out to the lake to fetch water, and letting downe the bucket to take vp water,by chance fell in himſelfe after it,and was preſently caried away by the ſtreame à bowes shoot from the ſide. This accident was at the ſame time reuealed to the man of God in his cell , who preſently called Maurus ſaying, Goe quickly Brother

B.5   Maurus,

Maurus, for the child who went to
fetch water is fallen in to the lake, and
the ftreame hath caryed him a great
way. A wonderfull thing and not
heard of fince the time of St. Peter:
Maurus hauing asked and receiued his
benediction vpon the command of his
Superiour, went forth in haft, and being
come to the place vpon the water to
which the childe was driuen by the
ftreame, thinking ftill he went vpon
dry land, tooke him by the haire of the
head , and retourned fpeedily back,
but no fooner had he foot vpon fi me
ground, but he came to himfelfe , and
looking back perceiued that he had
gone vpon the water, much aftonished,
and wondering how he had done that
which wittingly he durft not aduen-
ture. So retourning to the holy man,
he related what had happened , which
venerable Benedict afcribed to Maurus his prompt obedience, and not to
his owne merits ; but contrarywife
Maurus attributed it wholy to his co-
mand, not imputing the miracle to himfelfe

selfe which he had done vnwittingly.
This humble and charitable contentiō
the child who was saued, was to de-
cide, who said, when I was drawne
out of the water, methought I saw my
Abbots garment ouer my head, and
imagined that he had drawne me out.

Peter.

THese are wonderfull things you
report, and may be to the ædifica-
tion of many, and for my owne part the
more I heare of the good mans miracles, the more I desire to heare.

How a Crow caryed a way a poy-
sened loafe.

CHAP. VIII.

VVHen as now the places and
bordering Countries there-
about were very Zealous in the loue of
our Lord Iesus Christ, many aban-
doning the vanities of the world, and
putting

putting themselues vnder the sweet
yoake of our Redeemer (as it is the custome of the wicked to repine at the
vertues of otheres) one Florentius à
Priest of à church hard by, and grand
father to Florentius our subdeacon,
began by the instigation of the diuell
to oppose himselfe against the vertuous proceedings of the holy man: and
iniuriously to derogate from his course
of life, hindering also as many as he
could from resorting to him. But
seeing he could not stoppe his progresse,
the fame of his vertues still more encreasing, and many vppon the report
of his sanctity resoming their liues dayly ; he became far more enuious and
malitious ; for he desired himselfe the
commendations of Benedicts life, but
would not liue commendablely. Thus
blinded with enuy, he sent to the seruant of God à poysened lowfe of bread
for an offering; which the man of God
receued thankefully, although he was
not ignorant of the poyson in it. There
vsed to come to him at time of dinner à
crow

crow from the next forrest, which he
was accustomed to feed : comeing
therefore as she was wont, the man of
God cast before her the bread that the
Priest had sent him : saying I commande thee in the name of our Lord Ie-
sus-Christ to take this bread, and cast
where no man may finde it. The crow
gapeing & spreading her winges runne
croaking about it, as though she would
haue said, I would willingly fulfill thy
command, but I am not able. The man
of God commanded againe saying, take
it, take it vp, and cast it where no man
may find it. So at length shee tooke it
vp in her beake, and caried it aways &
twoe howres after retourned againe to
receiue from his hand her ordinare al-
louance. But the venerable father seing
the Priest so peruersely bent to seeke
his Life, was more sorry for him,
then fearefull of himselfe. When Florentius saw that he could not accomplish his wicked designe vpon the body
of his maister, he attempted to trie what
he could against the soules of his schol-
lars.

lars, in so much that he sent seauen
naked girles in to the garden of the
cloister in which Benedict liued, that
so playing lasciuiously hand in hand,
they might entice the Religious to
naughtines. Which when the holy man
espyed out of his cell, to preuent the
fall of his yong disciples, considering
that all this malice proceeded from hatred to him, he gaue place to enuy and
withdrewe himselfe. So after he had
disposed of the oratories and other buildings, leauing in them à competent
number of Brethren with Superiours,
he tooke with him à few Monkes, and
remooued to an other place. Thus the
man of God with humility auoided his
hatred, whom All mighty God stuke
with à terrible iudgement : for when
the foresaid Priest standing in his sum-
mar house to his great content and ioy,
vnderstood that the holy man was
gone, the roome wherin he was, fell
downe, crushed and killed him, all the
rest of the house remaining immoueable and entyre. This Maurus the
disciple

disciple of the man of God thought fitt to signifie forth with to Benedict who was yet scarce gone ten miles, willing him to retourne, for the priest who persecuted him was slaine. Which the mā of God hearing tooke very heauely; both because his enimie was dead, and because his Disciple reioyced thereat. Where vpon he enioyned him à penance for presuming in à ioyfull manner to bring such newes to him.

Peter.

THese are wonderfull strāge things, for in the drawing water out of à rock me thinks I behold in him Moyses, in raysing the iron from the bottome of the water he representeh Elysæus ; in walking on the water Peter, in the obedience of the crow I cōceiue him an other Helias, in bewayling his enemyes death, à Dauid. That man had vnited in him the spirits of all the iust.

Peter.

Gregory.

THe man of God Benedict had in
him (Peter) the spiritt of God a-
lone, which by the grace of free redemption replenished the harts of all
the elect, of which St. Iohn faith.
There was true light which illumina-
teth euery man that cometh in to this
world. Of which againe he writeth.
Of his plenitude and fulneſſe wee haue
all receiued : for the holy ones of God
could indeed receiue graces from God,
but they could not impart them to o-
thers. He then gaue miracles , or
ſignes of power to the lowely , who
promiſed that he would ſhew the miracle of Ionas to his enemyes, daigning
in their ſight to dye, and in the ſight of
the humb'e to ariſe. So that the one
ſhould haue what they would contemne, and the other what to reuerēce
and loue. By which myſtery was oc-
caſioned, that while the proud were
ſpectatours of his ignominious death,
the

the humble with glory might receiue
power against death.

Peter.

BVt declare I pray ; whither the
holy man remooued , or if he
wrought miracles in any other place.

Gregory.

THe holy man by remouing changed his habitation , but not his aduersary; for he edured their more sharpe
conflicts. For as much as he found the
authour of malice openly to assault
him . The castle called Cassine is si-
tuated vpō the side of à high mountaine,
which stretching forth in à forked
manner, enuironeth the same castell,
and riseth in to the aire three miles
high, on which stood an old temple
where Apollo was worshipped by the
foolish country people, according to
the superstitious custome of the ancient
heathens. Round about it likewise
grew

grew woodes and groues in which euē
vntill that time the paynims offered
their idolatrous facrifices. The man of
God comeing to this place, brake
downe the idoll, ouer threw the altar
burnt the groues, and of the temple of
Apollo made à chappell which he dedicated to St. Martine, & where the
profane altar had ftood, he built à
chapple of St. Iohn, and by dayly preaching conuerted many of the people
there about. But the old enemye incen-
fed with thefe proceedings, not
couertely, or obfcurely, but openly &
vifibly appeared in the fight of the father, and with hideous cries complained of the violence he fuffered in fo
much, that the brethren hard him, although they could fee nothing. For as
the venerable told his Difciples the
wicked fiend reprefented himfelfe to
his fight all on fire, and with flaming
mouth and flashing eyes; feemed to
rage againft him. And thē they all heard
diftinctly what the wicked fpiritt faid.
For firft he called him by his name, and
when

when the man of God would make
him no anſwer, he fell to raile and reuile him. And whereas before he cryed
Benedict, Benedict, and ſaw he could
get no anſwer; them he cryed maledict
not Benedict (that is curſed not bleſſed) what haſt thou to doe with me?
why doſt thou vexe me? But now we
ſhall behold new aſſaults of the enemye againſt the ſeruant of God, to
whom he miniſtred not ſo much com-
bats willingly, as occaſions of victory
againſt his will.

*How an huge ſtone by his prayer was
    made portable.*

Chap. IX.

ONe day as the Brethren were
    building the celles of the cloyſ-
ter, there lay a ſtone in the midſt which
they determined to lift vp, and put in to
the building; and when two or three
were not able to mooue it, they ſet more
to it; but it remained as immoueable as
                                    if it

if it had bine fixed in the ground, so that
it was easie to conceiue that the enemye sate vpon it, since that soe many
men were not able to lift it. After much
labour in vaine they sent to the man of
God with his prayers to driue away
the enemye, who presently came, and
hauing first prayed, made the signe of
the crosse ouer it, when behold, the
stone was as easely lifted as if it
had no waight at all.

*How the kitchin by the illusion of the
enemye appeared all
on fire.*

CHAP. X.

THen the man of God aduised the
Brethren to digge in the place
where the stone lay, when they had
entered à good deepenes, they found à
brasen idoll, which happening for the
present to be cast by in the kitchin,
presently there seemed à flame to rise
out

out of it, and to the sight of all the Brethren it appeared that all the kitchin
was on fire, and as they were cryeing
one to another, and casting water to
quench this fire, the man of God hearing the noise came, & perceiuing that
there appeared fire in the eyes of the
Brethren, and not in his, he presently
inclined himselfe to prayer, and called
vpon them whom he saw deluded with
an imaginary fire, willing them to signe
their eyes that they might beholde the
building entyre, and not that fantasti-
call fire which the enemye had coun-
terfaited.

How a boy crushed with the fall of a wall
was healed.

Chap. XI.

AGaine when the Brethren were
raysing the wall à litle higher for
more conuenience, the man of God
was at his deuotions in his cell, to whō
the enemye in an insulting manner appeared,

peared, and told him he was going to
his Brethren at worke; the man of God
ftraight waife by à meffenger aduerti-
fed the Brethren there of, warning thē
to haue à care of themfelues for the
wicked enimye was at that houre
come to moleft them. Scarce had the
meffenger told his errand, when the malignant fpiritt ouer threw the wall
that was à building, and with the fall
thereof bruifed à yong Monke, fonne
to à certaine Senatour. Hereat all of
them much grieued, and difcomfor-
ted, not for the loff of the wall; But for
the harme of their brother, brought
the heauy tideing to their venerable
Father Benedict, who bid them bring
the youth to him who could not be
carried but in à sheet, by reafon that
not onely his body was bruyfed, but
alfo his bones crushed with the fall.
Then he willed them to lay him in his
cell vpon his matte where he vfed to
pray : So caufeing the Brethren to goe
out he shutt the doore, and with more
then ordinary deuotion fell to his
                                    prayers.

prayers. A wonder to heare, the very
fame howre he fent him to his worke
againe whole and found as euer he was
before to helpe his Brethren in making
vp the wall ; whereas the enemie hoped to haue had occafion to infult ouer
Benedict by his death.

*Of Monks who had eaten out of
their Monastery.*

Chap. XII.

NOw began the man of God by
the fpiritt of prophecy to foretell
things to come, & to certifie thofe that
were prefent with him of things that
paffed far of. For it was the cuftome
of the Monaftery that the Brethren
fent abroad about any bufineff, should
neither eate, nor drinke, till their retourne , this in the practife of the rule
being carefully obferued, one day fome
Brethren vpon occafion went abroad,
and were forced to ftay later then
vfually , fo that they refted & refreshed
them-

themselues in the house of à certaine
deuout woman of their acquaintance.
Afterwards coming home very late,
they asked as was the custome the Abbots blessing. Of whom he streight
way demanded saying, where dined
you? they answered no where; he replyed, why doe you lye? did you not
goe in to such à womans house? eate
you not there such, and such meates?
dranke you not so many cuppes? When
the venerable Father had told them
both the womans lodging, the seuerall
sorts of meates, with the number of
their draughts. They all in great terrour fell downe at his feate, and with
acknowledgemēt of all they had done
confessed their fault, which he straight
wayes pardoned, perswading himselfe
they would neuer after attempt the
like in his absence, knowing he was
alwayes present with them in spiritt.

*How he reprooued the Brother of Valen-
tinian the Monke for eatinge by
the way.*

CHAP. XIII.

MOreouer the Brother of Va-
lentinian the Monke, whom
wee mentioned in the beginning, was
very deuout although but à Sæcular,
he vſed euery yeare once to goe from
his dwelling to the Monaſtery, & that
faſting, that he might partake of the
prayers of the ſeruant of God, and ſee
his Brother. As he was in his way an
other trauayler who caryed meate
with him put himſelfe in to his company, and after they had trauayled à good
while he ſaid to him. Come Brother
let vs refresh ourſelues, leaſt wee faint
in the way. God forbid (anſwered the
other) by no meanes Brother, for I
neuer vſe to goe to the venerable Father Benedict but faſting. At which
anſwer his fellow trauayler for the
C   preſent

present said no more; when they had
gone à litle farther, he moued him a-
gaine, but he would not consent , because he resolued to keepe his fast. So
the other was à while silent , and went
on forward with him, after they had
gone a great way wearied with long
trauaille , in their way they came to à
meadow, and à spring with what else
might delight them there to take their
repast. Then said his fellow trauayler
loe here is water, heere is à meadow,
here is à pleasant place for vs to refresh
and rest vs à while, that we may without endangering our health make an
end of our iourney. Soe at the third
motion (these words pleasing his eare,
and the place his eye) he was ouer
come, consented and eate. At the euening he came to the Monastery, where
conducted to the venerable Father he
craued his benediction and prayers. But
presently the holy man reprooued him
for what he had done in the way saying,
what was it Brother that the malignant enemye suggested to thee in
                                    the

the way by thy fellow traueller. The
first time he could not preuaile, nor yet
second, but the third time he preuailed,
and obtained his desire. Then the man
acknowledging his fault, and frailty,
fell at his feete more sorry for his offence by reason that he perceiued he
had offended althogh absent in the
sight of Father Benedict.

Peter.

I Discouer in the breast of the holy
man, the spirit of Heliseus which
was present with his disciple far
of him.

*How he discouered the dissimulation
of king Totila.*

CHAP. XIV.

Gregory.

BE silent Peter with patience that
you may vnderstang strange:
C 2   thin.

things. For in the time of the Gothes, their king informed that the holy man had the gift of prophecy : as he went towards his Monastery he made some stay à litle way of, and gaue notice of his coming, to whom answer was made from the Monastery, that he might come at his pleasure; the king of à treacherous nature attempted to trye, wheter the man of God had the spirit of prophecy. There was one of his followers called Riggo, whom he caused to put on his royall robes and buskins on his feete, and so commanded him taking on him the kings person to goe forward towards the man of God, three of his cheife pages attending vpō him, to witt Vsiltike, Roderike, and Blindine, to the end they should waite vpon him in the presence of the seruant of God, that so by reason of his attendance, and purple robes he might be taken for the king. When the said Riggo with his braue apparell and attendance entred the cloister, the man of God sate a far of, and seing him come
so nie

foone as he might heare his voice, he cryed to him, faying, putt of fonne, putt of that thou carieft it is not thine. Riggo ftraight waies fell to the ground fore abafhed for hauing præfumed to delude the holy man, all his followers likewife fell downe aftonifhed, and rifeing they durft not approach vnto him, but retourned to their king, and trembling related vnto him how foone they were difcouered.

How Benedict by prophecy foretold the king, and Bifhop of Canufina future euents.

CHAP. XV.

AFter this, king Totila came him-felfe to the man of God, whom fo foone as he faw fitting à far of, he durft not come nigh, but fell proftrate to the ground, the holy man twice or thrice bad him rife, but he durft not get vp, then the holy man came himfelfe to the king & lifted him vp and fharply

C 3   re-

reprehendet him for his wicked
deedes, moreouer he foretold him in
few words what should befall him.
faying, much mifcheife haft thou done,
much wickedneff haft thou committed, at leaft now giue ouer thy iniquity. But I forefee thou wilt enter into
Rome, thou wilt paff the feas, raigne
nine yeares, and dye the tenth. At the
hearing whereof the king fore apal-
led, craued his prayers, and departed,
from that time forward he was leff
cruell, and not long after he went to
Rome, thence fayled in to Sicely, and
the tenth yeare by the iuft iudgement
of God loft both life & crowne: moreouer the Bishop of the Dioceffe of
Canufina vfed to come to the feruant
of God and for his vertuous life was
much refpected. He conferring with
him concerning the comeing of Totila,
and the taking of the city of Rome.
The city doubteleffe (faid the Bishop)
wil be fo fpoiled, and difpeopled by
this king, that it will neuer more be in
habited. To whom the man of God
                                    anfwe-

anſwered, Rome (ſaid he) ſhall neuer be deſtroyed by the paynimes ; but with lightning, tempeſt, and earth-quakes ſhall decay in it ſelfe. The veritie of which prophecy is already ſufficiently manifeſted, for in this city wee ſee the walles ruined, houſes ouerturned, and churches throwne downe with tempeſtuous windes, and we may obſerue buildings to decay, and dayly fall to ruine. Although Honoratus his diſciple (from whoſe relation I had it) told me he heard it not himſelfe, from his owne mouth, but was told it by the Brethren.

How venerable Benedict for à time diſpoſeſſed à certaine Clearke from the Diuell.

Chap. XVI.

AT that time one of the cleargie of the church of Aquine was moleſted with à wicked ſpirit whom the venerable man Conſtantius Biſhop

C 4 of

of that Dioceſſe had ſent to diuers
Martyrs shrines to be cured; but the
holy Martyrs would not free him, that
the gifts of grace in Benedict might be
made manifeſt . He was therefore
brought to the ſeruant of Allmighty
God Benedict, who with prayers to our
Lord Ieſus-Chriſt preſently droue out
the enemie. Hauing cured him he co̅-
manded him ſaying. Goe, and hereafter neuer eate fleſh, and præſume not
to take holy orders, for what time
ſoeuer you shall præſume to take holy
orders, you shall againe become ſlaue
to the diuell. The Clearke therefore
went his way, and (as preſent puniſh-
ments make deepe impreſſions) he
carefully for à while obſerued this co̅-
mande. But when after many yeares
all that were aboue him therein holy
orders were dead, ſeeing alſo his infe-
riors to be promoted before him by
reaſon of their holy orders , he grew
careleſſe, and forgetfull of what the
man of God had ſo long agoe ſaid vnto
him, ſo that he likewiſe went, and re-
                                    ceiued

ceiued priest hood when presently the
diuell who before had left him, againe
tooke power of him, and never ceased
to torment him till he seuered his soule
from his body.

Peter.

THe holy man I perceiue vnderstood the secret decrees of God,
in that he knew this Clearke to be deliuered to the power of the enemie, lest
he should præsume to receiue holy
orders.

Gregory.

VVHy should not he know
the secrete decrees of the diuine prouidence, who kept the commandements of God, sith it is written
that *he who adheereth to God is one spirit
with him.*

Peter.

IF he who adheereth to our Lord become one spiritt with him, how comes the same excellent Preacher to say: *who hath knowne the minde of our Lord, or who hath bin his counsellour?* for it seemes altogether vnlikely that he who is made one with an other, should not know his minde.

Gregory.

HOly men so far as they are one or vnited with God are not ignorant of his ordinances as the same Apostle saith. *For what man knoweth the things of à man, but the spirit of à man that is in him?* So the things also that are of God no man knoweth, but the spirit of God. And to shew that he knew the things of God he addeth. *And we haue receiued not the spirit of this world, but the spirit that is of God.* And againe *that eye hath not seene, nor*

care

eare hath neard, neither hath it ascended in to the heart of man what things God hath prepared for those that loue him; but to vs God hath reuealed by his spirit.

Peter.

IF then those thing which appertained to God were reuealed to the said Apostle by the spirit of God. What meaneth he to make this præamble saying. *O depth of the riches of the wisdome and knowledge of God: how incomprehensible are his iudgments, and his wayes vnsearcheable?* But as I am saying this, another quæstion ariseth: for the Prophet Dauid saith to our Lord. *In my lippes I haue vttered all the iudgments of thy month.* And whereas it is lesse to comprehend or know, then to pronounce, what is the reason St. Paul should affirme that the iudgements of God are incomprehensible, and Dauid professeth not onely to know them, but also with his lippes to expresse them?

Gre.

Gregory.

TO both these difficulties, I briefe-
ly answered before when I said,
that holy men (so far as they are one
with God) are not ignorant of the
mind of our Lord : for all that deuoute-
ly seeke God, in their deuotion, and
contemplation, are with God, but in
regard they are depressed with the
waight of this corruptible body, they
are not wholy with God, and therefore
for as muchas they are vnited with God
they know his secret iudgements, of
which likewise they are ignorant, for
as much as in respect separated from
him : And so they professe his iudgements incomprehensible which they
can not as yet thoroughly vnderstand.
But they who in spirit adheere vnto
him, in this adhæsion to God know his
iudgements either by the sacred words
of scripture, or by hyden reuelations,
so far as they are capable ; these therefore they know and declare, but they
are

are ignorant of those which God concealeth. Wherevpon the Prophet Dauid when he had said *in my lippes I will pronunce all thy iudgments*, immediately addeth *of thy mouth*, as if he had said plainely. Those iudgments I could both know, and pronounce which thou didst tell me, for those which thou speakest not, thou concealeth from our knowledge. Thus the saying of the Prophet agrieth with that of the Apostle, for the iudgments of God are both incomprehensible, & also those which proceed from his mouth are vttered with the lippes of men, for being so manifested they may be both conceiued and expressed by men, nor can they be concealed.

Peter.

BY occasion of the difficulty I propounded, you haue explicated and reconciled the testimonies alleadged, but if there remaine ought concerning the vertue of this Man I pray declare it.

How

*How S. Benedict foretold the destruction
of his Monastery.*

Chap. XVII.

Gregory.

A Certaine noble man named
Theoprobus was by this holy
Father S. Benedict conuerted from the
pleasures of the world to the Seruice
of God, who for his vertuous life was
very familiar, and intimate with him.
He entering one day in to the holy
mans cell found him weeping bitterly,
and when he had expected à good
while, and saw he did not giue ouer
(although it was his custome in prayer
mildely to weepe, and not to vse any
dolefull lamentations) he boldely demanded of him the cause of so great
greife. To whom the man of God presently replyed. All this Monastery I
haue built with what soeuere I haue
prepared for my Brethren, is by the
iudg-

iudgment of Allmighty God deliuered
to the heathens: and I could scarse obtaine to saue the liues of the monkes
in this place; His words Theoprobus
heard; But wee see them verified in
the destruction of his Monastery by
the Longobardes. For of late these
Longobardes by night when the Religious were at rest, entred the Monastery, and ransacked all, yet had not
the power to lay hand on any man. But
Allmighty God fulefilled what he had
promised to his faithfull seruant Benedict, that although he gaue their goods
in to the hands of the paynims, yet he
præserued their liues. In this blessed
Benedict did most clearely resemble S.
Paul whose ship with all its goods
being lost, it pleased God to bestow
vpon him the liues of all those who
were with him.

HoW.

How S. Benedict *discouered the hiding of* à *Flagon of wine.*

CHAP. XVIII.

OVr Monke Exhilaratus whom
you know well, on à time was
sent by his maister with two wooden
vessels (we call flagons) full of wine
to the holy man in his Monastery. He
brought one, but hid the other in the
way not withstanding the man of
God although he was not ignorant of
any thing done in his absence, receiued
it thankefully, and aduised the boy as
he was retourning back in this manner; Be sure childe, thou drinke not of
that flagon which thou haft hid, but
turne the mouth of it downeward, and
then thou wilt perceiue what is in it;
He departed from the holy man much
ashamed, and desirous to make further
triall of what he had heard, held the
flagon à side and presently there came
forth à snake, at which, the boy was
sore

fore afrighted, and terrified for the euill he had committed.

How the man of God reprooued à Monke for receiuing certaine napkins.

CHAP. XIX.

NOt farr diſtant from the Monaſtery was à certaine towne, in which no ſmall number of people by the moueing exhortations of Benedict were conuerted from their ſuperſtious idolatry. In that place were certaine religious women, and the ſeruant of God Benedict vſed to ſend often ſome of his Brethren thither to inſtruct and edifie their ſoules. One day as his cuſtome was he appointed one to goe; But the monke that was ſent after his exhortation tooke of the Nunnes ſome ſmall napkins, and hid them in his boſome. As ſoone as he came back the holy Father beganne very ſharpely to rebuke him ſaying : How hath iniquity

quity entred thy breaſt : The monke
was amazed , and becauſe he had for-
gott what he had done , he wondred,
why he was ſo reprehended. To whom
the holy Father ſaid. What? Was not
I preſent when thou tookeſt the napkins of the hand maids of God , and
didſt put them in thy boſome? where
vpon he preſently fell at the feete of
the holy man , and repenting his folly
threw away the napkins which he had
hidde in his boſome.

How the man of God vnderſtood the
proud thought of one of his
Monkes.

Chap.   XX.

ONe day as the venerable Father
late in the euening was at his re-
paſt, it happened that one of his mōkes
who was ſonne to à lawyer held the
candle to him : and whileſt the holy
man was eating he ſtanding in that
manner beganne by the ſuggeſtion of
                                    pride

pride to say with in himselfe. Who is
he whom I should waite vpon at table, or hold the candle vnto with such
attendance ? Who am I who should
serue him? To whom the man of God
presently turning checked him sharpely saying; signe thy breast Brother,
what is this you say ? make the signe of
the crosse on your breast. Then he forth
with called vpon the Brethren ; and
willed them to take the candle out of
his hande, and bad him for that time to
leaue his attendance , and sit downe
quietly by him. The monke being asked afterward of the Brethren concerning his thoughts at that time, con-
felfed to them how he was puffed vp
with the spirit of pride, and what con-
temptible words he harboured in his
thought against the man of God. By
this it was easely to be perceiued that
nothing could be kept from the knowledge of venerable Benedict, who was
able to penetrate the very secret
thoughts of the heart.

Of

Of two hundred bushels of meale mira-
culously brought to the Monas-
tery gate.

Chap. XXI.

AT another time also in the country of Campania began à great
famine, and great scarcety of victualls;
so that all the wheate in Benedict his
Monastery was spent, and but fiue
loaues of bread remained for the Bre-
threns refection. When the venerable
Father perceiued them sad, and discon-
tented, he endeauored by à milde and
gentle reproache to reprehend their
pusillanimitie, and with faire promises
to comfort them saying: why are you
sad for want of bread? to day you are
in want, but to morrow you shall haue
plenty. The next day there were found
two hundred sacks of meale before
the Monastery gates, by whom God
Allmighty sent it as yet no man knoweth. Which when the monkes beheld

held they gaue thankes to God and by this were taught in their greatest want to hope for plenty.

Peter.

BVt refolue I pray, is it to be thought that this feruant of God had continually the fpiritt of prophecy, or onely at certaine times with fome difcontinuance?

Gregory.

THe fpirit of prophecy Peter doth not alwayes caft his beames vpon the vnderftanding of the prophets; for as it is written of the holy Ghoft. *He breatheth where he will* ; fo likewife muft we conceiue alfo when he pleafeth. And therefore Nathan being demanded by the king if he might builde the temple , firft aduifed him to doe it, afterward forbad him. This was the reafon that Helyzæus knew not the caufe why the woman wept ; but said

said to his seruant. *Who did oppose her, let her alone, for her soule is in anguirh, & our Lord hath concealed it from me, and not made it knowne.* Thus God Allmighty of his great mercy disposeth with singular prouidence; to the end that by giuing the spirit of prophecy some times, and at other times withdrawing the same, the mindes of the Prophets be both eleuated aboue théselues; and also be truely humbled, for by receiuing the spirit they may know they are inspired by God, and againe when they receiue it not, they may consider what they are of themselues.

Peter.

IT standeth with good reason what you haue said ; but I beseech you prosecute whatels you remember of the venerable Father Benedict.

*Ho*w

*How by à Vision he gaue order to con-
triue à Monastery.*

Chap. XXII.

AN othertime the holy Father was
requested by à certaine deuout
man to send some of his disciples to
build à Monastery in à mannourie of
his neare the city Tarracina ; to which
request he condescended , and made
choise of his monkes whom he sent,
appointing them an Abbot with à
Prouost, and as they were setting forward on theyr iourney he spake to the
saying : Goe, and vpon such à day I
will come, and shew you where to cō-
triue the oratory , where the refectory,
and lodging for guests , or what els
shall be necessary. So they receiued his
blessing and departed in hope to see
him at the appointed day , for which
they præpared all thinges they thought
fitt , or necessary for their venerable
Father and his company. The night
before

before the appointed day, the man of
God appeared in sleepe to him whom
he had constituted Abbot and to his
Prouost, and described to them most
exactely how he would haue the building ordered. And when they a waked
they related to each other what they
had seene: yet not altogether relying
vpon that vision, they expected the
holy man according to his promise,
but seeing he came not at his appointed
time, they retourned to him very pen-
siue saying: wee haue expected (Father)
your comming as you promised, but
you came not to shew vs where and
what we should build. The holy man
answered. Why Brethren? Why doe
you say so? Did not I come according
to my promise? And when said they,
came you? Did not I replyed he, appeare to each of you in your sleepe, &
described euery place? Goe and according to the direction was giuen you in
that vision, contriue the Monastery. At
these wordes they were much asto-
nished, and so retourning to the man-
nour

nour they erected the building according to the reuelation.

Peter.

I Would gladly be informed how
and in what manner he could ex-
preſſe his mind to them ſo far of ; ſo
that they ſhould both heare, and vnderſtand by an apparition.

Gregory.

VVHat is the reaſon, Peter,
thou doeſt ſo curiouſly
ſearch out the manner how it was
done? It is euident that the ſpirit is of
à more noble and excellent nature then
the body. And we are taught by the
ſcripture how the Prophet was taken
vp in Iury, and ſet downe with the
dinner he carried with him in Chaldee;
who after he had refreſhed an other
Prophet with his victuals found himſelfe againe in Iury. If then Abacuc in
à momét could corporally goe ſo farre,

      D   and

and carry his dinner; what wonder if
the holy man obtained to goe in spirit,
& intimate to the spirits of his brethrē
what was necessary? That as the other
went corporally to conueigh corporall
foode, so he might goe in spirit to in-
forme them of things concerning à
spirituall life.

Peter.

I Confesse by this your discourse
you haue giuen full satisfaction to
my doubt, yet I would gladly know
what kind of man he was in his common conuersation.

*How certaine Religious women were
absolued after their
death.*

Chap. XXIII.

EVen his ordinary discourse (Peter)
had à certaine efficatious vertue,
for

for his hart being eleuated in contemplation, would not let à word passe
from him in vaine. Nay if at any time
he had vttered any thing by way of
threatning, rather then determining,
his wordes had the same force and effect as if he had absolutely decreed it.
For not far from his Monastery two
Nunnes of noble race and parentage
liued in à place of their owne, and a
certaine religious man prouided them
all things for the exteriour; but as in
some, nobility of birth causeth basenes
in mind, so that those who beare in
mind their owne greatnes, do lesse
humble themselues in this world: these
foresaid Nunnes had not as yet refrai-
ned their tongues by à religious habit,
but by their vnaduised speches oftentimes prouoked to anger the good
man who had care ouer them. Wherefore after he had for à long time endu-
red their contumelious language, he
complained to the holy man of the in-
iuryes he suffred; which as soone as
the man of God heard, he commanded

them

them forth with saying : haue care of
your tongues, for if you doe not a-
mend, I excommunicate you : which
sentence of excōmunication not w.th-
standing he did not pronounce, but
threaten.   Yet for all this they nothing changed in their former condi-
tions, within à few dayes after, departed this life, and were buryed in the
church, at such time as in the church à
solemne Masse was soong, and the
deacon (as the custome is) cryed a-
lowd : if there be any that communi-
cateth not, let him goe forth : then the
Nurse of the two virgins (who vsed
to make offeringes to our Lord for
them)saw them rise out of their graues,
and goe forth.   This she obserued
sundry dayes, that alwayes when the
Deacon cryed in that manner, they
went out not able to remaine in the
church, and calling to mind what the
man of God had said vnto them, whilst
they were liuing (for he excluded them
from communion vnlesse they amended their language and manners) she
                                    with

with great sorrow informed the seruant of God what she had seene who presently with his owne hands gaue offering, and said : goe , and cause this oblation to be offered to our Lord , and they shall be no longer excommunicated. When therefore this offering was made , and the Deacon according to the ceremony cryed out, that such as did not communicate should goe out of the church they were not seene to goe forth any more ; whereby it was apparent ; that whereas they went not forth with the excommunicated , they were admitted by our Lord to communion.

Peter.

IT is merueilous strange that this venerable and holy man as yet liuing in this mortall life, should be able to release those who were vnder the inuisible tribunall.

Gre-

Gregory.

ANd was not he (Peter) in this
mortall life to whom it was said:
*whatsoeuer thou shalt binde vpon earth,
shall be also bound in heauen, and whatsoeuer thou shalt vnbind on earth, shall
be also vnbound in heauen.* Whose place,
and autority in binding, and loofeing
they poflefse, who by faith and vertuous life obtaine the dignity of holy
gouernment. And that man (an earthly
creature) might receiue this foueraigne
power; the Creatour of heauen, and
earth came downe from heauen, and
for the redemption of man kinde, God
himfelfe became man, that this spirituall power might be granted to flesh.
For fo Allmighty God condefcending
(as it were) beneath himfelfe, raifed
our weakenes abowe it felfe.

Pe-

Peter.

HIs miraculous power is confirmed with good reason.

How à Boy was cast out of his
graue.

Chap. XXIV.

ON à time à certaine younge
Monke of his, who was ouer
much affected towards his parents,
went out of the Monastery without
his benediction; and the very same
day as soone as he was come to them,
he died, and being buried, the day following they found his body cast vp,
which they enterred the second time,
and the next day after it was found in
like manner lying aboue ground as
before. Heere vpon they ran streight-
way, and fell at the feete of the most
        D 4   milde

Father Benedict imploring his aide.
to whom the man of God with his
owne hand gaue an hoft of the bleſſed
Sacrament, ſaying. Goe, and with all
reuerence lay this hoft of the body of
our Lord vpon his breaſt, and ſo bury
him. This done the earth kept his
body, and neuer after caſt it vp. By this
you perceiue (Peter) of what merit
this man was with our Lord Ieſus.
Chriſt , ſith the very earth caſt forth
the body of him who had not receiued
the bleſſing of Benedict.

Peter.

I Doe plainely perceiue it, and am
much aſtonished therat.

Of a

Of à Monke who leauing his Mo-
naftery met à Dragon in
the way.

CHAP.   XXV.

Gregory.

ONe of his Monkes of a wandering, and vnconftant difpofition would by no meanes abide in the
Monaftery. And although the holy
mã had often reprooued, & admonished him of it, he remained deaf to all
perfwafions, and oftentimes entreated
earneftly to be releafed from the con-
gre gation. So the holy Father ouercome with this importunity in anger
bid him be gone. Scarfe was he got
out of the Monaftery, when he met in
the way à Dragon that with open
mouth made towards him, and feeing
it ready to deuoure him, he beganne to
quake, & tremble crying out alowde
helpe, helpe, for this Dragon will de-

D 5   uoure

uoure me. The Brethren vpon this
fuddain noyfe ranne out; yet faw no
Dragon, but found the Monke pan-
ting, and afrighted; fo they brought
him back againe to the Monaftery,
who forth with promifed neuer to
depart from the Monaftery; and from
that time he remained alwayes conftant in his promife, as who by the
prayers of the holy man was made fee
the Dragon ready to deuoure him,
which before he had followed vndif-
couered.

*How St. Benedict cured à boy of
the leprofy.*

CHAP.   XXVI.

I Will alfo relate what I heard of à
very honorable man named Antho-
nie, who affirmed that à feruant of his
Father fell into à leprofie, in fo much
that his haire fell of, and his skinne was
fwolne, fo that he could noe longer
hide the deformity of his difeafe dayly
                                increa-

increasing. This seruant was sent by
the gentlemans Father to the man of
God, and by him restored to his perfect health.

How St. Benedict miraculously procured
money for à poore man to dis-
charge his debt.

CHAP. XXVII.

NOr will I conceale that, which
his Disciple Peregrine was wont
to relate, how an honest poore man
constrained by necessity of à debt,
though his onely remedie was to haue
recourse to the man of God; So he came
to the monastery, where meeting with
the seruant of God, he told him how
he was extreamely vrged by his credi-
tour for the payment of twelue shillings. The venerable Father answered him, that in very deed he had not
twelue shillings, but yet he comforted
his want with good wordes saying:
goe, & after two dayes retourne hither
againe;

againe; for at this present I haue it not
to giue you. These two dayes as his
custome was he spent in prayer; and
vpon the third day, when the poore
debter came againe, there was found
thirteene shillings vpon à chest of the
Monastery, that was full of corne,
which the man of God caused to be
brought him, and gaue them to the
distressed man, that he might pay
twelue, and haue one to defray his
charges. But to retourne to the relation of such things as I learned of his
disciples of whom I spake in the beginning. There was à certaine man had
an aduersary, who bare him deadely
hatred, and so great was his malice
that he gaue him poison in his drinke,
which potion although it procured not
his death, yet it so altered his colour
that his body became all speckled like
à leapour. This man was brought to
the holy Father, who by his onely
touch, caused the diuersity of colours
to vanish away, and restored him to his
health.

How

How a glasse bottle cast downe
vpon stones was not
broken.

Chap. XXVIII.

AT such time as the great famine
was in Campania, the man of
God gaue all he had to those he saw in
want and necessity; in so much that
there was no prouision almost left in
the spence, saue onely à litle oyle in à
glasse vessell; yet when one Agapitus
à subdeacon came humbly entreating
to haue à litle oyle giuen him, the man
of God (who had resolued to giue all
vpon earth, that he might haue all in
heauen) commanded this litle oyle
that was left to be giuen him. The
Monke who was dispencier heard his
command, but was loath to fulfill. And
the holy man à litle after demanded
whether he had done what he willed
him, the Monke answered that he had
not giuen it, saying that if he should
haue

haue giuen that , there would be nothing left for the Religious; hereat the
good Father much difpleafed, bad fome
other take the glaffe bottle in which
there remained à little oyle & caft it
out of the window , that nothing of
the fruits of difobedience might be left
to pefter the Monaftery; which was
accordingly done: vnder the window
was à fteepe fall full of huge rough
ftones, vpon which the glaffe fell, yet
it remained as whole, and entyre as
if it had not bin throwne downe, fo
that neither the glaffe was broke, nor
the oyle fpilt ; which the man of God
commanded to be taken vp and giuen
to him that asked it. Then calling
the Monkes together he rebuked the
Religious man before them all for his
pride,& want of confidence.

How

How an empty tunne was filled with oyle.

Chap. XXIX.

HAuing ended the chapter he and all the Monkes fell to their prayers. In the place they prayed was an empty tunne cloſſe couered. As the holy man continued his prayer the couer of the ſaid tunne beganne to be heaued vp by the oyle encreaſing vnder it, which runne ouer the brim of the veſſel vpon the floore in great abundance. Which ſo ſoone as the ſeruant of God Benedict beheld, he forth with ended his prayer, and the oyle ceaſed to runne ouer. Then he admoniſhed the diſtruſtfull, and diſobedient Monke to haue confidence in God, and learne humility. So the Brother thus reprehended was much aſhamed, becauſe the venerable Father did not onely by word admonish him; but alſo did miraculouſly show the power of
Allmighty

Allmighty God. Nor could any man
afterwardes doubt of what he promised, sith as it were in à moment : for à
glasse bottle almost empty he had restored à tunne full of oyle.

How he dispossessed à Monke.

CHAP. XXX.

ONe day as he was going to S.
Iohns chappell, which stands
vpon the very toppe of the mountaine,
he mette the subtill enemie vpon à
mule in the habit, and comportment of
à physitian , carryeing à horne , and à
morter, who being demanded whither
he went, answered he was going to
the Monkes to minister à potion. So
the venerable Father Benedict went
forward to the chappell to pray, and
haueing finished retourned backe in
great hast,for the wicked spirit found
one of the ancient Monkes drawing
water, and præsently he entred into
him, threw him downe, and tortured
him

him pittifully. As foone as the holy man retourning from prayer found him thus cruelly tormented , he onely gaue him à blow on the cheeke with his hand , and immediately draue the wicked fpirit out of him, fo that he durft neuer after retourne.

Peter.

I Would know whether he obtained thefe great miracles alwayes by prayer , or did them fometimes onely by the intimation of his will.

Gregory.

T Hey who are perfectly vnited with God as neceffity requireth, worke miracles both wayes; fometimes by prayer , fometimes by power ; for fith according to St. Iohn, *As many as receiued him , he gaue them power to be the children of God* ; what wonder is it if they haue the priuiledge, and power to worke miracles who are
                                        exalted

exalted to the dignity of the children of God. And that both wayes they worke miracles is manifest in St. Peter, who by prayer raysed Tabitha from death; and punished with death Ananias and Saphira for their falshood. For we doe not read that he prayed when they fell downe dead; but onely that he rebuked them for their fault committed. It is euident therefore that these things are done sometimes by power, sometimes by petition; sith that by reproofe he depriued these of their life; and by prayer reuiued the other. But now I will produce two other acts of the faithfull seruant of God Benedict, by which it shall appeare euidently, that some things he could doe by power receaued from heauen, and others by prayer.

*How St. Benedict loosed à Husbandman
by his onely sight.*

Chap. XXXI.

A Certaine Goth named Galla,
was of the impious sect of the A-
rians. This fellow in the time of their
king Totila was most malitiously bent
against all good, and deuout catho-
lickes; in so much that if any clargie
man, or monke came in his sight, he
was sure not to escape aliue from him:
This man enraged with an insatiable
couetousnes of spoile, and pillage, light
one day vpon à husbandman whom he
tortured with seuerall torments; the
man not able to endure the paine, professed that he had comitted his goodes
to the custody of the seruant of God
Benedict, this he faigned to the end he
might free himselfe from torments, and
prolong his life for some time. Then
this Galla gaue ouer tormenting him,
and tying his armes togeather with à
strong

ſtrong corde, made him runne before
his horſe, to ſhew him who this Benedict was that had receiued his goodes
to keepe. Thus the poore man runne
before him with his handes bounde, &
brought him to the holy mans Monaſtery, whom he found ſitting alone at
the Monaſtery gate, and reading. Then
the countryman ſaid to Galla who followed furiouſly after him : loe this is
the holy man Benedict, whom I told
you of. The barbarous ruffian looking
vpon him with enraged fury, thought
to afright him with his vſuall threats,
an with hydeous noiſe cried out vnto
him riſe, riſe, and deliuer vp this fellowes goodes which thou haſt taken
into thy cuſtody. At theſe clamorous
wordes the man of God ſuddainely lifted vp his eyes from reading, and ſaw
him with the huſbandman whom he
kept bound, but as he caſt his eye vpon
his armes, in à wonderfull manner the
cordes beganne to fall of ſo quickly,
that no man could poſſibly haue ſo
ſoone vntyed them. When Galla perceiued

ceiued the man whom he brought
bound so suddainely loosened, and at
liberty, strooke in to feare at the sight
of so great power he fell prostrate, and
bowing his stiff, and cruell neck at the
holy mans feete, begged his prayers.
Not with standing the holy man rose
not from his reading, but called vpon
his brethren to bring him to receaue
his benediction; when he was brought
againe vnto him, he exhorted him to
leaue his barbarous and inhumane
cruelty. So pacified by the holy mans
admonition, he departed neuer after
presuming to aske any thing of the
country man, whom the man of God
vnloosed not by touching, but by casting his eye vpon him. Thus you see
(Peter) as I said before that those who
are the true seruants of Allmightie God,
sometimes doe worke miracles by à
commanding power; for he who sitting still abated the fury of that terrible Goth, and with his onely looke
vnloosed the cordes where with the
innocent mans armes were fast pinio-
ned,

sheweth euidently by the quick, and speedy exhibition of the miracle, that he wrought it by à power receiued, & actually refideing in him. Now I will alfo shew you how great, and ftrange à miracle he obtained by prayer.

How he rayfed à dead man
to life.

Chap. XXXII.

AS he was one day in the field labouring with his Brethren, à certaine peafant came to the Monaftery caryeing in his armes the dead body of his fonne, and with pittifull lamentation for the loffe of his onely fonne, inquired for the holy Father Benedict. Vnderftanding that he was in the field, he prefently laid downe the dead corps at the Monaftery gate, and as one diftracted through griefe, beganne to runne to finde out the venerable Father. At the fame time the man

of

of God was coming home with his
Brethren from labour, whom when
the distressed man espyed, he cryed out
vnto him, Restore me my sonne, Restore me my sonne. At the hearing here-
of the man of God made à stop, and
said: what freind haue I taken your
sonne from you? The man replyed he
is dead, come, and rayse him. When
the holy man heard this, he was much
agreiued, and said, Goe Brethren, goe,
this is not à worke for vs but for such
as were the holy Apostles. Why will
you impose burdens vpon vs which we
cannot beare? Not withstanding the
man enforced with excessiue greife,
perseuered in his earnest petition, swea-
ring that he would neuer depart vntill
he raysed his sonne to life. Then the
man of God demanded saying where
is he? He answered: his body lieth at
the Monastery gate. Whither when
the man of God with his Brethren was
come, he kneeled downe, and layed
himselfe on the body of the child:
then raysing himselfe with his hands
held

held vp towards heauen he prayed : ô
Lord regard not my sinnes but the
faith of this man who craueth to
haue his sonne restored to life, and restore againe to this body the soule
which thou hast taken from it. Scarse
had he finished these wordes, but all
the body of the child beganne to treble
at the reentry of the soule, that in the
sight of all who were present, he was
seen with wonderfull quakeing to
pant & breath whom he presently
tooke by the hand, & deliuered him
à liue & sound to his Father. It seemeth
to me (Peter) he had not this miracle
actually in his power, which he pros-
trated himselfe to obtaine by prayer.

Peter.

VV Hat you haue said is vn-
doubtedly true, for you effectually proue,& confirme by deedes
what was said in wordes. But (I pray)
certifie me, whether holy men can effect,

fect, and obtaine what so ere they will, or desire.

Of the Miracle wrought by his sister Scholastica.

CHAP. XVII.

Gregory.

VVHo was euer (Peter,) in this life more sublime in perfection, & sanctitie chan. St. Paule, who not with standing three times craued of our Lord to be free from the motions of the flesh, yet could not ob-taine it? To this purpose I must tell you à passage concerning the venerable Father Benedict, that there was some thing he desired, and was not able to accomplish. His sister Scholastica who was consecrated to God from her very childehood, vsed to come once à yeare to see him; vnto whom the man of God was wont to goe to à house not far frō the gate with in the possession of the

E   Monas-

Monaſtery. Thither she came one
day according to her cuſtome, and her
venerable brother likewiſe with his
diſciples, where after they had ſpent
the whole day in the prayſe of God,
and pious diſcourſes, the night drawing on, they tooke their refection
together. As they were yet ſetting at
table, and protracting the time with
holy conference, the vertuous, and
Religious virgin his ſiſter began to
importune him ſaying: I beſeech you
(good Brother) leaue me not this
night, that we may entertaine ourſelues vntill next morning in diſcourſes
of the ioyes of heauen. To whom he
anſwered. What is this you ſay, ſiſter?
by no meanes can I ſtay out of my
Monaſtery. At this time the sky was
very cleare, and not à cloud was to be
ſeene in the ayre. The holy Nunne
therefore hearing her Brothers deniall,
layed her hands vpon the table faſt clo-
ſed together, and vpon them inclined
her head to make her prayer to Allmighty God : As she rayſed vp her
head

head againe from the table, on à sud-
dain beganne such vehement lightning, and thunder ; with such aboun-
dance of raine that neither venerable
Benedict, nor his Brethren were able
to put foote out of doores. For the holy
virgin when she leaned her head on
her hands , powred forth à flood of
teares vpon the table, by which she
changed the faire weather into foule,
and rainy. For immediately followed
that inundation of waters , and such
was the coherence with her prayers,
and the storme; that as she lifted vp her
head, the cracke of thunder was heard;
as if the rayfing vp of her head, and the
bringing downe thefe floodes of raine
had concurred in one and the fame in-
ftant. The holy man perceiuing that by
reafon of thunder , and lightning with
continuall showres of raine , he could
not poffibly retourne , was in great an-
guish of mind, and faid vnto her : God
Allmighty forgiue you (fifter) what is
this you haue done ? she repleyed , I
made my requeft to you, & you would

not heàre me; I prayed to Allmighty
God, and you fee he hath granted it.
Now therefore if you can goe forth to
the Monaſtery, and leaue me.   But he
not able to retourne was forced to ſtay
againſt his will.   Thus it ſo fell out
that they ſpent the night in watching,
and receiued full content in ſpirituall
diſcourſe of heauenly matters. By this
it appeares (as I ſaid before) that the
holy man deſired ſome thing which he
could not obtaine. For if we conſider
the intent of the venerable Father,
without quæſtion he would haue had
the faire weather to continue in which
he came forth. But it pleaſed Allmighty God, by meanes of à woman miraculouſly to cauſe the contrary. And
noe wonder if at that time, à woman
were more powerfull then he, conſide-
ring she had à long deſire to ſee him;
and therefore ſith as St. Iohn affirmeth
God is charity with good reaſon she
was more powerfull who loued more.

P̧ɛ-

Peter.

I Grant it, and am wonderfully taken with your difcourfe.

How St. Benedict faw the foule
of his fifter in forme of
à doue.

CHAP. XXXIV.

THE next day the holy, and Religious virgin went home to her cloifter, and the man of God to his Monaftery. Three dayes after ftanding in his cell, he faw the bleffed foule of his fifter depart out of the body, and in forme of à doue afcend, and enter into the cæleftiall manfions. Wherefore with ioy congratulating her heauenly glory, he gaue thankes to God in hymnes, and prayfes, and ftraightwayes certified his Brethren of her departure, whom he forthwith fent to bring her body to the Monaftery, and caufed it

to

to be buryed in the same tombe that he
had præpared for himselfe. To the end
their bodies might not be separated by
death, whose mindes were alwayes v-
nited with God.

How the whole world was represented be-
fore his eyes : And of the
soule of German Bis-
hop of Capua.

Chap.   XXXV.

AN other time Seruandus Deacō,
and Abbot of that Monastery
(which was built by Liberius sometime
à senatour in the country of Campania) vsed often to visit him ; for being
also illuminated with grace, and heauenly doctrine, he repaired diuers times
to the Monastery, that they might mu-
tually communicate one to an other
the wordes of life, and at least with
sighes, and longing desires, taiste of
that sweet food of the cælestial country , whose perfect fruition they were
not

not as yet permitted to enioy. And now the time of rest being come, venerable Benedict went vp to the hygher roome of the tower, and Seruandus had his lodging in the lower, from which there was an open passage to ascend to the hygher, and ouer against the said tower was à large building in which the disciples of both reposed while as yet the Monkes were at rest, the seruant of God Benedict riseing before to the night office, stood at the window, and made his prayer to Allmighty God about midnight, when suddainely he looked forth, and saw à light glancing from aboue so bright, & resplendent, that it not onely dispersed the darkenes of the night, but shined more cleare then the day it selfe. This was à merueilous strange vision, for (as he afterwardes related) the whole world compacted as it were together, was represented to his eyes in one ray or sunne beame. As the venerable Father had his eyes fixed vpon this glorious lustre, he beheld the soule of Ger-

E 4   manus

manus Bishop of Capua caryed by Angels to Heauen in a fiery globe. Then for the teſtimony of ſo great a miracle, with a lowd voice he called vpon Seruandus the Deacon twiſe, or thrice by his name, who much aſtoniſhed thereat, came vp, looked forth, and ſaw a litle ſtreame of the light then diſapearing, at the ſight wereof he was ſtrooke into great admiration; and the man of God after he had related to him the whole paſſage, ſent preſently to Theoprobus à Religious man in the caſtle of Caſſine, willing him to goe the ſame night to Capua, and enquire what had happened to the Biſhop Germanus. And it fell out ſo, that he who was ſent found the moſt Reuerend Biſhop Germanus dead; & inquiring more exactely, he learned that his departure was the very ſame moment in which the man of God had ſeene him aſcend.

Pe-

Peter.

THis was à ſtrange, and admirable
paſſage; but whereas you ſaid the
whole world was at one view repre-
ſented to his ſight, as I neuer expe-
rienced the like, ſo I cannot imagine
how, or in what manner this was poſ-
ſible, that the whole vniuerſe ſhould
be ſeene at once, and by one man.

Gregory.

TAke this Peter for an aſſured ve-
rity, that to à ſoule that beholdeth
the Creatour, all creatures appeare but
narrow; for ſhould we partake neuer
ſo litle of the light of the Creatour,
what ſoeuer is created would ſeeme
very litle, becauſe the ſoule is enlarged
by this beatificall viſion, and ſo dela-
ted in the Diuine perfections, that it far
tranſcendes the world, and it ſelfe alſo.
The ſoule thus rapt in the light of God,
is in her interiour lifted vp, and enabled
aboue

aboue it felfe, and while thus eleuated
it contemplates it felfe , it eafely com-
prehendet how litle that is which before it was not able to conceiue. So the
Bleffed man who in the tower faw that
fiery globe with the Angels retourning
to heauen, could not poffibly haue beheld thefe things, but onely in the light
of God. What wonder then if he faw
the world at one view , who was in
mind exalted aboue the world.   But
whereas I faid that the whole world
compacted as it were together was reprefented to his eyes, it is not meant
that heauen , and earth were ftreigte-
ned by contraction , but that the mind
of the beholder was dilated , which
rayfed to the fight of Allmighty God,
might eafely fee all things beneath
him. It followeth therefore , that the
exteriour light which appeared to his
fenfes, proceeded from an inward illu-
mination of mind , by which he was e-
leuated to hygher mifteries , & taught
how meanely thefe inferior things are
to be efteemed.

Pc-

Peter.

I Blame not now my ignorance
which hath bin the occasion of so
large, and profitable discourse : But
since you haue clearely explicated these
things vnto me, I pray, goe forward
with your discourse.

*How St. Benedict wrote à Rule
for his Monkes.*

Chap. XXXVI.

I Would willingly (Peter) relate
more concerning this holy father,
but that I must of purpose omit many
things to speake of the acts of others;
onely this I would not haue you to
be ignorant of, that the man of God a-
mongst so many miracles where with
he shined to the world, was also very
eminent for his doctrine; for he wrote à
Rule for Monkes as cleare in stille, as
excellent for disc.etion. And if any man
desire

defire to know more exactely the life,
and conuerfation of this holy F..her,
he may there behold it as in à mir our:
for the Bleffed man could not poffibly
teach otherwife then he liued.

How he prophetically foretold his death to his Brethren.

CHAP.   XXXVII.

THe fame yeare in which he departed out of this life, he foretold the
day of his death to fome of his Difciples who conuerfed with him, and to
others who were far of, giueing ftrict
charge to thofe who were prefent, to
keepe in filence what they had heard;
and declaring to the abfent by what
figne they should know when his foule
departed out of his body. Six dayes before his departure, he caufed his graue
to be opened, and immediately after he
fell into à feuour, by the violéce where
of his ftrength began to decay, and
the

the infirmity dayly encreasing, the sixt-
day he caused his Disciples to carie
him in to the oratorie. Where he armed himselfe with the pretious body
& bloode of our sauiour , then sup-
porting his weake limbes by the
armes of his Disciples , he stood vp his
handes lifted towards heauen and with
wordes of prayer breathed forth his
holy soule. The very same day two of
his Disciples, the one liueing in the
Monastery, the other in à place far remote, had à reuelation in one , and the
selfe same manner. For they beheld à
glorious way spred with pretious garments , and enlightned with innume-
rable lampes, stretching directly east-
ward from his cell vp to heauen. A
man of à venerable aspect stood a-
boue, and asked them whose way
that was, but they professing they
knew not: This saith he, is the way
by which the beloued of God Benedict ascended. Thus as the Disciples who were present saw the departure

parture of the holy man ; ſo alſo thoſe who were abſent , vnderſtood it by this ſigne foretold them. He was buryed in the oratorie of St. Iohn Baptiſt which himſelfe had built vpon the ruines of Apolloes altar. In the caue alſo in which he formerly liued, euen to this day miracles are wrought vpon ſuch as repaire thither with true faith.

How a madde woman was cured in St. Benedict his caue.

C H A P. XXXVIII.

FOr very lately happened this which I now relate. A certaine woman bereft of reaſon , and alto-geather diſtracted in her ſenſes, runne madde ouer mountaines , and val-lies, through woodes, and plaines, day and night , neuer reſting , but when ſhe was forced for wearieſome-
neſſe

nesse to ly downe ; one day as she ranged thus madly vp, and downe, she light vpon the caue of Blessed Benedict, and by chance entred, and remained there : The next morning she came out as sound, and perfect in her senses, as if she neuer had bin out of them, and from that time remained all her life in health, and quiet of mind, which she there recouered.

Peter.

VVHat should be the reason that we experience euen in the patronages of martyrs that they doe not bestow so great fauours by their bodies, as by some of their reliques ; yea and doe greater miracles where their bodyes are not ; at least not whole, and entyre?

Greg

Gregory.

VV Here the bodyes of holy Martyrs lye no doubt (Peter) but there they are able to shew many miracles, as they doe. For to such as haue recourse vnto them with pure intention, they shew many maruellous fauours. But in regard weake soules may doubt whether they be present to heare them or no, in such places where men know their whole bodyes are not: it is necessary for confirmation of their presence to shew more miracles were the weake of faith may haue occasion to doubt. But they who doe stedfastly beleeue in God , encrease their merit in that, although theire bodyes lye not there , yet they assure themselues to be heard by them. Wherefore Trueth it selfe to encrease the faith of his Disciples said, vnto them : *if I goe not the Paraclete shall not come to yon.* For where as it is vn-
doubtedly

doubtedly certaine, that the Holy
Ghost the comforter alwayes procee-
deth from the father, and the sonne;
why doth God the sonne say, he will
goe from them that the Paraclete may
come who neuer departeth from the
sonne? But because the Disciples con-
uersing with our Lord in flesh, did
desire alwayes to behold him with
their corporall eyes it was rightly
said vnto them : *vnlesse I goe away
the Paraclete shall not come.* As if he
had said plainely : If I withdrawe
not my bodily presence, I doe not
shew you the loue of the soule ; and
vnlesf you cease to see mee carnally,
you shall neuer learne to loue me spi-
ritually.

Peter.

YOu say well.

Gregory.

NOw let vs reſt awhile; that by ſilence we may be the better enabled for further conference, if we intend to proſecute the miracles of other Saints.

The ende of the ſecond booke of the life of St. Benedict.

F I N I S.

The approbation of the Rule giuen by St. Gregorie the great.

I Gregorie Prelat of the holy Roman sea, wrote the life of Blessed Benedict: I haue read the Rule which the Sainct himselfe wrote with his owne handes. I prayſed it, and confirmed it in à holy ſynod: I commanded it to be moſt diligently obſerued by all who shall be admitted to the grace of conuerſion through diuers parts of Italy whereſoeuere the Latin tongue is read, euen to the ende of the world. I doe alſo confirme the twelue Monaſteries which the Sainct erected.

THE RVLE

OF OVR MOST HOLIE FATHER

S. BENEDICT

PATRIARCHE

OF MONCKES

THE PROLOGVE
OF OVR MOST
HOLY FATHER
St. BENEDICT TO

HIS RVLE.

ARKEN ô sonne to the precepts of a maister, and incline the eare of thy hart willingly to heare the admonition of a pious father and effectually accomplish them. That by the labour of obedience thou maist returne to him from whom by the slouth of disobedience thou hast departed. To thee therfore now my speech is directed who renouncing thy owne will, being to fight vnder

A   ou

our Lord Chriſt the true kinge takeſt to thee the moſt ſtrong and bright armour of obedience.

First of all that what good thinge ſoeuer thou beginſt to doe, thou begge of him with moſt earneſt praier to perfect it : that he who hath now vouchſafed to reckon vs in the number of his children may not herafter be contriſtated by our ill deeds : for wee muſt ſoe at all times ſerue him with the goods he hath beſtowed vpon vs, that neither as an angry father he may not herafter diſinherit his children; nor as a dreadfull Lord exaſperated by our offences deliuer vs ouer as wicked ſeruants to perpetuall punishment , who would not follow him to glory.

Let vs therfore at length ariſe the ſcripture exciting vs , and ſaying; It is now the houre to riſe from ſleepe. And our eyes being opened to the deifying light , let vs with aſtonished eares heare what the diuine voice daily cryeing out, admonisheth vs ſayeing, This day if you ſhall heare his voyce, harden

den not your harts. And againe; He that hath eares let him heare what the spirit saith to the Churches : and what saith it? Come children, heare mee; I will teach you the feare of our Lord. Runne whilest you haue the light of life, least the darknes of death surprize you.

And our Lord seeking his labourer amongst the multitude to whom here he speaketh, sayeth againe, Who is the man that will haue life, and desireth to see good dayes? which if thou hearing answerest; I. God saith vnto thee; If thou wilt haue true and euerlasting life, refraine thy tounge from euill, and thy lips that they speake not guile, Decline from euill, and doe good : Seeke after peace and pursue it. And when you haue done this, my eyes shall be vpon you; and my eares shall be open to your prayers, and before you can call vpon me, I will say, Behold I am present. What thing deare brethren can be more sweet vnto vs, then this voyce of our Lord inuiting vs? Behold our Lord

A 2   through

through his piety sheweth vnto vs the
waye of life.

Our loynes therefore being girt
with faith and the obſeruance of good
workes, and our feet shodde by guidāce
of the Ghoſpell of peace let vs walke
in his wayes, that wee may deſerue to
ſee him who hath called vs vnto his
kingdome. In the tabernacle of whoſe
Kingdome if wee deſire to dwell, wee
muſt apply our ſelues to good workes
which is the only meanes wherby it is
to bee attained. But let vs aske our
Lord with the Prophet ſayeing vnto
him; Lord who shall dwell in thy tabernacle, or who shall reſt in thy holy
hill? After this queſtion brethren let
vs heare our Lord anſwering; and
shewing vs the waye that leades to his
tabernacle, ſaying. He that walketh
without ſpott, and worketh iuſtice.
He that ſpeaketh truth in his hart, that
hath not forged guile in his tongue. He
that hath not done euill to his neighbour, and hath not receiued reproch a-
gainſt his neighbour. He that reiecting
out of his minde the malignant Deuill,

with

with all his suggestions hath brought
them all to nought, and hath taken his
beginning thoughts and dasht them a-
gainst Christ,

They who feare our Lord doe not
take pride in their good obseruance and
well doing, but knowing that all the
good they haue, or can doe, proceedes
not from themselues, but is done by
our Lord, magnifie our Lord thus
workinge in thē, sayinge with the Prophet; Not to vs Lord not to vs, but to
thy name giue glory. So Paule the A-
postle did not impute any thinge of his
preaching to himselfe saying by the
grace of God I am what I am. And a-
ganie he saith. He that gloryeth let him
glory in our Lord; And here vpon also
our Lord saith in the Ghospell. He that
heareth these my words, and perfor-
meth them, I will liken him to a wise-
man, that hath built his house vpon
a roche. The floods came, the winds
blew, and beate against that house, and
it fell not; because it was founded
vpon a rocke. Our Lord fulfilling
these things, expecteth dayly that wee

should by deeds anſwer to theſe his holy admonitions.

Therefore for the amendment of our euills, he prolonges the dayes of this our life according to the words of the Apoſtle ſaying, Knoweſt thou not that the patience of God bringeth thee to repentance? For our pious Lord ſaith, I will not the death of a ſinner but rather that he be conuerted and liue. Hauing therfore my brethren demanded of our Lord, who should be the Inhabitour of his Tabernacle, we haue hard what his duty and charge is; which if we fulfill, we ſhall be Inheritours of his heauenly Kingdome.

Now Therefore let vs prepare our harts and bodyes to fight vnder the holy obedience of his commandes, and what nature in vs is not able to performe, let vs begge of our Lord to ſupply it with the aſſiſtance of his grace. And if wee deſire to avoyde the paines of Hell, and to attaine to euerlaſting life; whileſt yet time ſerues, and whileſt wee liue in this mortall fleſh, and that wee may performe all theſe things by the light of
Grace,

Grace, let vs haſten and doe that now,
which may be expedient for vs for euer
hereafter. Wee are therefore now to
inſtitute a ſchoole of the ſeruice of God.
In which ſchoole or inſtitution wee
hope nothing ſhall be ordained too ri-
gourous or burdenſome. But if in ſome-
thinges we proceede with à litle ſeueri-
ty, reaſon ſo requiring, for the amendment of vices or preſeruing of charity,
do not ſtraightwayes for feare there of
fly from the way of ſaluatiō, which is always ſtraight and difficult in the beginning. But in proceſſe and continuance of
this holy courſe and conuerſation, the
hart being once dilated, the way of
Gods commandements is runne with vn
ſpeakable ſweetnes of loue : ſo as neuer departing from his ſchoole, but per-
ſeuering in the monaſtery in his doctrine vntill death, by patience wee parti-
cipat of the ſufferings of Chriſt, that
wee may deſerue afterwards to bee partakers of his kingdome. Amen.

Heare

Of the seuerall kindes, or life of Monkes.

Chap. I.

IT is well knowne that there are foure kindes of Mōkes. The first is of Cœnobites, that is monasteriall or conuentuall liuing vnder a Rule or Abbot. The second kinde is of Anachorits, that is, Hermits, who not by à Nouitiall feruour of deuotion but by long probation in a monasticall kinde of life haue learnt by the comfort and encouragement of others to fight against the Deuill, and being well armed, secure now without the help of any are able by Gods assistance to fight hand to hād against the vices of the flesh and euill cogitatiōs; and soe proceed frō the fraternall army to the single cōbat of of the wildernes. The third and worst kinde of Mōks are the Sarabaits who hauing not beene tryed vnder any Rule, by the experience of a skilfull maister, as gold vseth to be tryed in the furnace; but softned according to the nature of

lead,

lead, by their workes adhering yet to the world, are knowne by their tonsure to be disloyall to God: who two or three or perhaps single without a shepheard are shut vp, not in our Lords sheepfolds but in theire owne : and the pleasure of their desiers is to them a lawe, and whatsoeuer they like or make choise of, this they will haue to be holy, and what they mislike, that not to be lawfull. The fourth kinde of mõks be those which are called Girouagi or wanderers, who all their life time wander through diuers prouinces, and guestwise stay two or three days in one Monastery, and then in another, and are allways wandering and neuer setled, and giuing themselues alltogether to their owne pleasures, and to the inticements of gluttony, are generally in all things worse then the Sarabaits. Of the miserable conuersation of all which, it is better to be silent then to say much. And therfore leauing these, let vs by Gods assistance set downe a Rule for Cœnobits or Conuentualls which is the principall sort of all.

A 5

What

What kind of man the Abbot ought to bee.

CHAP. II.

AN Abbot who is worthy to haue charge of a monastery, ought allways to remember what he is called, and to expresse in his actiōs the name of Antient. For in the monastery he representeth the person of Christ, seing he is called by his name or title, as the Apostle saith. Ye haue receiued the spirit of adoption of children in which wee cry abba father. And therfore the Abbot ought to teach ordaine or cōmand nothing but what is conformable to the commandes of our Lord (and God forbid he should do otherwise) But let his commands and doctrine be mingled in the mindes of his disciples, with the leauen of the diuine iustice. Let the Abbot allways be mindefull that in the dreadfull iudgement of God he is to giue account both of his doctrine, and of the obedience of his disciples. And

let

let him know that it will be found the
shepheards fault, what want of profit
soeuer the maister of the family shall
find in his sheep : But if he haue be-
stowed all diligence on his vnquiet and
disobedient flocke, and haue employed
the vttermost of his care for curing of
their corrupt manners, then shall he be
discharged in the iudgement of our
Lord, and may say with the Prophet,
I haue not hidden thy iustice in my hart,
I haue told thy truth and thy saluation:
but they contemning despised me. And
then finally death as a iust punishment
shall be inflicted vpon the disobediet
sheepe.

When therfore any one taketh vpō
him the name of an Abbot, he ought to
gouerne his disciples with a twofold
doctrine, that is, To shew them all vertue and sanctity more by deeds then by
words : and to capable disciples he may
declare the commandements of God by
words, but to the hard harted persons
and to such as are more simple, he must
shew them by his actions and life.
And all things which he shall teach his
disci-

difciples to be vnfitting, by his owne a-
ctions let him shew that they ought
not to be done : leaft preaching well to
others, hee himfelfe be foud reprobate,
and God fay vnto him finning. Why
doeft thou declare my iuftices, and ta-
keft my teftament in thy mouth, Thou
haft hated difcipline and haft caft my
fpeeches behind thee. And, Thou who
haft feene a moate in thy brothers eye,
haft not feene a beame in thy owne. Let
there be no acception of perfons in the
monaftery. Let not one be loued or
fauoured more then an other, except
fuch a one as in good workes and obedience shall be found to furpaffe others.
Let not a free mā or of better parentage
coming to Religion, be preferred before him who is of feruile or meaner
condition, except there be fome other
reafonable caufe for it. But if vpon iuft
confiderations the Abbot shal foe think
fitting let him doe it, in any rancke or
degree what foeuer, otherwife let euery
one keepe their owne places. Becaufe
whether bondman or free man, wee
are all one in Chrift, and beare an e-
                                    quall

quall burthen of feruitude vnder one
Lord; for with God there is noe accep-
tiõ of perfons. Onely in this he maketh
a difference, if in good workes and humility wee furpaffe others.

Therefore let the Abbot beare e-
quall loue towards all : and let all be
fubiect to the fame orders , and difcipline according to their deferts. For the
Abbot ought allwayes in his doctrine
to obferue that Apoftolicall forme
where it is fayd , Reprooue, intreate, reprehend, that is; tempering, as times and
occafions require, faire fpeeches with
terrours: Let him fhew both the feueri-
ty of a maifter, and the pious affection
of a father: that is, he ought fharply to
reproue fuch as are difordered and vnquiet , and of the other fide to deale by
intreaty with fuch as ar obedient mild
and patient, exhorting them to goe forwards in vertue. But by all meanes the
negligent and contumacious perfons let
him feuerely reprooue and chaftife.

Let him not diffemble the finnes of
delinquēts, but as foone as they appeare,
let him vfe all poffible endeuour vtterly.

terly to roote them out, remembring
the danger of Hely Prieſt of Silo. The
more honeſt and vnderſtanding diſpo-
ſitions let him for the firſt and ſecond
time admonish by words ; but the
ſtubborne, hard harted, proud and diſobedient, euen in the very beginning of
ſinne, let him chaſtiſe with ſtripes, and
bodily punishment, knowing that it
is written. The foole is not corrected
with words. And againe; Strike thy ſone
with the rod, and thou shalt deliuer his
ſoule from death.

The Abbot ought always to remember, what he is, and what he is called,
and that to whom more is committed,
from him more is exacted. And let
him conſider what a difficult and hard
taske he hath vndertaken, to gouerne
ſoules, and to accommodate himſelf to
the humors of many. Whereof ſome
ar to be led by faire ſpeeches, others by
sharp reprehenſions, and others by
perſwaſions. Therefore let him ſoe
conforme himſelf to each one according to their quality and vnderſtading,
that he may not onely ſuffer noe loſſe in
the

the flock committed to him, but may also reioyce in the increase and profit of his vertuous flocke.

Aboue all things let him take heede least he dissemble or litle regard the saluation of the soules committed to him, and haue more care of transitory and worldly things : but let him alwayes consider that he hath vndertaké the gouernment of soules, of which he is also to giue an account. And that he may not complayne for want of temporall meanes let him remember what is written. Seeke first the kingdome of God and his iustice, and all these thinges shall be giuen v nto you. And againe, Nothing is wanting to such as feare him. And let him know that he who vndertakes the gouernment of soules must prepare himselfe to giue an account of them. And what the number of brethren vnder his care is, let him certainly know that at the day of Iudgment he is to giue an account to our Lord of ail their soules besides the accout he is to giue for his owne. And soe alwayes fearing the future account of

a pa-

a paſtour for the flock committed to
his charge, whilſt he is ſollicitous for
other mēs accounts, he is alſo made care
full of his owne. And whilſt he reclay-
meth others by his admonitions, himſelfe is freed from vices.

*Of calling the Brethren to
counſell.*

CHAP. III.

AS often as any principall matter
is to be donne in the monaſtery,
let the Abbot call togeather all the cōgregation, and let him declare what the
matter is. And hearing the counſell of
his brethren, let him conſider prudently
with himſelfe, and doe what he ſhall
iudge moſt expedient. And the reaſon
why wee ordaine that all be called to
counſell, is becauſe our Lord often re-
uealeth to the younger, that which is
beſt. And let the brethren giue counſell
with all ſubiection and humility, and
not preſume ſtifly to defend their owne
opinions, but let them refer it to the
                                    Abbots

Abbots difcretion; and what he shall thinke expedient, to that let them all fubmit. And as it belongeth to the difciples to obey their maifter; fo it behoueth him to difpofe all things prouidently and iuſly. In all thinges therefore let all follow the Rule, as their miftris, and let no man rashly fwarue from it. Let none in the monaftery follow their owne wills. Neither let any one prefume with in or with out the monaftery peruerfly to contend with his Abbot: which if he doe, let him be fubiect to regular difcipline: Not with ftanding let the Abbot doe all thinges with the feare of God, and obferuance of the Rule, knowing that he shall udoubtedly giue an accout of all his iudgements, to God our moft iuft Iudge. And if any lefter thinges are to be donne for the benefit of the Monaftery, let him onely vfe the counfell of the Seniours, as it is written. Doe all thinges with counfell and thou shalt not afterwards repent thee of it.

Which

Which bee the instruments of good
workes.

Chap. IV.

First of all to loue our Lord God
with all his hart, with all his soule
with all his strength. Then his neighbour as him selfe. Then not to kill. Not
to commit adultery. Not to steale. Not
to couet. Not to beare false witnesse. To
honour all men. And what he will not
haue donne to himselfe let him not doe
to another. To deny himselfe to himselfe that he may follow Christ. To
chastize his body. Not to seek after de-
lights. To loue fasting. To releeue the
poore. To cloth the naked. To visit the
sicke. To bury the dead. To help those
that are in tribulation. To comfort the
sadd. To withdraw himselfe from
worldly businesses. To preferre nothing
before the loue of Christ. Not to giue
waye to anger. Not to beare reuenge in
his mind. Not to foster guile or deceipt
in his hart. Not to make fayned peace.
                                    Not

Not to forsake charity. Not to sweare
at all, least perhaps he forsweare himselfe. To speake the truth from hart and
mouth. Not to doe euill for euill. Not
to doe any injury. Yea and patiently to
suffer an injury donne. To loue his enemyes. Not to speake ill of such as speake
ill of him, but rather to speake well
of them. To suffer persecution for iustice. Not to be proud. Not a louer of
wine. Not a great eater. Not drowsie.
Not slouthfull. Not a murmurer. Not
a detracter. To put his trust in God.
Whē he shall see any good thing in himselfe, let him attribute it to God, not to
himselfe. But let him always know
that euill is donne by himselfe, and therfore let him attribute it to him selfe. To
feare the daye of iudgement. To be af-
fraid of Hell. To desier life euerlasting
with spirituall thirst. To haue death always before his eyes. To obserue euery houre the actiōs of his life. To know
for certaine that God beholdeth him
in euery place. Presently with the remembrance of Christ to put away euill
thoughts entering into his hart, and to
                              reueale

reueale them to his spirituall father. To keepe his mouth frō euill and naughty words. Not to loue much talking. Not to speake vaine words and such as mooue laughter. Not to loue much and dissolute laughter. Willingly to heare holy readings. To praye often deuoutly. To confes dayly to God in praier euills past, with tears and sighes. To amend those euills for the time to come. Not to fullfill the desiers of the flesh. To hate his owne will. To obey the commandements of the Abbot in all things, although he himselfe (which God for bid) should doe other wise, being mindefull of that precept of our Lord, what they saye doe yee : but what they doe, doe yee not. Not to desier to bee called holy, till he be soe, and first to be soe, that he may truly becalled. so. Dayly to fullfill in deeds, the commaundemēts of God. To loue chastity. To hate noe man. To fly enuie and emulation. Not to loue contention. To fly haughtines. To reueren-

his

his elders. To loue his inferiours for Chrift his fake. To praye for his eni-myes. To make peace with his aduer-fary before the fetting of the fonne. And neuer to difpare of Gods mercy. Behold thefe are the inftruments of fpirituall profeffion , which things when they fhall night and day con-ftantly be performed by vs, and layd open in the day of Iudgement , that re-ward fhall be giuen vs in recompence by our Lord , which he hath promi-fed, that eye hath not feene , nor eare heard , nor hath afcended in to the hart of man, what God , hath pre-pared for thofe that loue him. The woike houfe where all thefe things are to be done , is the cloyfter of the monaftery and ftability in the Con-gregation.

Of

Of the obedience of the disci-
ples.

Chap. V.

THe first degree of obedience is obedience without delay. This besee-
meth those who esteeme nothing more
deare to them then Christ, by reason of
the holy profession they haue made, or
for the feare of Hell, or glory of life e-
uerlasting. Presently as soone as any
thinge shall be commanded them by
the superiour, as if it weare commanded
by God, they make noe delay in doeing
it. Of whom our Lord saith; From the
hearing of the eare he hath obeyed me.
And to Superiours and teachers he saith.
He who heareth you heareth me, therefore such persons as these leauing presently all their owne occasions and for-
sakeing their owne will, casting out of
their hands and leauing imperfect what
they were about, with the speedy foet
of obedience follow with deeds the
voice of the commander. And as it were
in

in one moment the command of the maister, and the perfect worke of the disciple in the feare of God, goe both jontly together, and are speedely effected by those who thirst after life euerlasting. These take the narrow way of which our Lord saith; Narrow is the way which leadeth to life, not liuing according to their owne will or following their owne desiers and pleasures; but liuing in monasteries, and hauing an Abbot ouer them, walking according to his directions & commandes. With out doubt such as these imitate that sentence of our Lord where he saith; I came not to doe my owne will but the will of him who sent me. And This obedience will thē be acceptable to God and pleasing to men, if that which is commanded be done, not fearefully, slowly, coldly, or with murmuration, or with an answer shewing vnwillingnes. Because the obedience which is giuen to superiours is giuen to God, who hath said. He who heareth you heareth me. And it ought to be done of the disciples with a good will: because God ioueth

a chear

a chearfull giuer. If the disciple obey with an ill will and shall murmur not onely in words, but also in his hart, though he fulfill what is commanded him, it will not be acceptable before God, who considereth the hart of the murmurer. And for such a worke he shall not get reward, but rather incurreth the penalty of murmurers, if he doe not amend and make satisfaction.

Of Silence.

Chap. VI.

LEt vs doe according to the sayeing of the Prophet. I haue said I will keepe my wayes, that I offend not in my tongue. I haue been watchfull ouer my mouth. I haue held my peace and humbled my selfe and been silent from speaking good thinges. If therfore some times according to this saying of the Prophet for silence sake we are to abstaine from good talke; how much more ought we to refraine, for the
guilt

guilt and penalty of finne from euill words. Therfore for the grauity of filence let leaue of fpeaking feldome be-giuen, euen to perfect difciples, though of good and holy matters and tending to edification. Becaufe it is written. In much fpeaking thou shalt not efchew finne. And in another place. Death and life in the hands of the tongue. For it behoueth a maifter to fpeake and teach, and it be feemeth a difciple to holde his peace and heare. Therfore if any thing be to be asked of the Priour let it be done with all humility fubiec-tion and reuerence, that they may not feeme to fpeake more then is ne-ceffary. But fcurrilities or idle words and fuch as moue laughter, we vtterly condemne and forbid in all places. And doe not permitt a difciple to open his mouth to fuch fpeeches.

Of

Of Humility.

CHAP. VII.

THe holy scripture cryeth to vs
brethren saying, Euery one who
exalteth himselfe shall be humbled, and
he who humbleth himselfe, shall be
exalted. Hereby declaring vnto vs,
that all exaltation, is a kinde of pride,
which the Prophet sheweth how
carefully he auoyded, saying; Lord
my hart is not exalted neither are my
eyes lifted vp; neither haue I walked in
great things, nor in wonders aboue my
selfe. But what? If I did not thinke
humbly but haue exalted my soule: As
a child weaned from his mother, soe
wilt thou reward my soule. Wherfore
brethren, if we will attaine to true humility, and will speedily come to that
heauenly exaltation to which we ascéd
by the humility of this present life; by
our ascending actions that ladder is
to be set vp which appeared to Iacob
in

in his sleepe, where he saw Angels
descending and ascending. That descēt
and ascent signifieth nothing else, but
that wee descēd by exalting our selues.
and ascend by humbling our selues.
And this ladder thus erected is our life
here in this world, which by humility
of hart is lifted vp to heauen by our
Lord; And the sydes of this ladder we
vnderstande to be our body and soule,
in which the diuine maiesty hath placed diuers degrees of humility, & discipline to be ascended.

The first degree of Humility.

THe first degree of hnmility is to
haue always the feare of God before his eyes, and not to forgett himselfe
But to be still mindefull of all thinges
that God hath commanded : & to remember that such as contemne God,
fall into hell for their sinnes ; and that
euerlasting life is prepared for such as

feare

feate him. And foe to keepe himfelfe
from all finne & vice of thought, word
eyes, hands, feet and proper will; and
foe fpeedely cut of all fleshly defiers.
Let him thinke himfelfe to be always
beheld from heauen of God; and all his
actions, where foeucr he be, to ly open
to his diuine fight , and to be prefented to God euery howre by his
Angells. The Prophet declareth this
when he saith God to be allways prefent to our thoughts in thefe words,
God fearcheth the hart and reynes
And, Our Lord knoweth the thoughts
of men that they are vaine. And a-
gaine, Thou haft vnderftoode my
thoughts a fare of. & The thought of
man shall confefle to thee. Let therfore
the humble brother , that he may be
catefull to auoid euill thoughts, allways faie in his hart. Then shall I be
with out fpott before him, if I shall
keepe me from my iniquity. The Scripture alfoe forbiddeth vs to doe our
owne will faying, Leaue thy owne will
& defire. And befides we begge of God
in

in our daily praier that his will may be done in vs.

We are taught therefore with good reaſon to take heede of doing our owne will, the ſcripture ſaying. There are wayes which ſeeme right to mē, the end where of plungeth euē into the deepe pitt of hell. And againe ſpeaking of negligent perſous; They are corrupted and made abominable in their pleaſures. And in the deſiers of the fleſh wee ought to beleeue God to be alwayes preſent to vs, according to that of the Prophet ſpeaking to our Lord. Before thee is all my deſire. Let vs then take heed of ill deſires, becauſe death is neare to the entrance of delight, whereupon the ſcripture commandeth. Follow not thy concupiſcences. If therefore the eyes of our Lord behold both good & bad, and our Lord always lookes downe from heauen vpon the ſonnes of men, to ſee who is vnder ſtanding or ſeekeing God; and that our workes are by our Angells Guardians daye & night told to

our.

our Lord and maker; We muſt alwaystake heed, Brethren, leaſt (as the Prophet in the Pſalme ſaieth) God ſometymes behold vs declining to euill & become vnprofitable : and though he ſpare vs for the preſent becauſe he is mercifull and expecteth our conuerſion and amendment, leaſt he ſay to vs hereafter, Theſe thinges thou haſt done & I haue held my peace.

The ſecond degree of humility is, If not louing his owne will he ſeeke not to ſatisfie his deſiers, but imitate that ſaying of our Lord, I came not to doe my owne will, but the will of him who ſent me. The ſcripture likwiſe ſaieth; The will hath puniſhment, and neceſſity purchaſeth à crowne.

The third degree of humility is, If for the loue of God he ſubmit himſelfe with all obedience to his ſuperiour, imitating our Lord of whom the Apoſtell ſayth, He was made obedient euen to death.

The fourth degree of humility is, If that in obedience hard and contrary
thinges

thinges & also iniurious beinge done
to him, he imbrace them patiently
with a quiet conscience; and suffering
growe not wearye, and giue ouer, according to that of the scripture, Who per-
seuereth vntill the end he shall be saued. And againe, let thy hart be comforted & expect our Lord. And shewing that the faithfull man ought for
our Lord to beare all thinges, though
neuer so contrary, he sayth in the person of the sufferers. For thee we suffer
death all the daye longe: wee are estee-
med as sheep of the slaughter. And
being assured by hope, of a reward at
Gods handes they goe on reioycing &
saying, But in all these thinges, we ouercome by the help of him who hath
loued vs. And likewise in another place the scripture saith. Thou hast proued
vs o Lord : thou hast tried vs with fire
as siluer is tried. Thou hast brought
vs into the snare; Thou hast laid tribulation vpon our backs. And to
shew that we ought to be vnder a
Prior or superiour he followes on
B 4 saying.

saying. Thou haſt placed men ouer
our heads, Fulfilling alſo by patience
the precept of our Lord in aduerſityes
& iniuries, being ſtruck on the one
cheeke they offer the other : leaue
their cloakes to him who takes awaye
their coate;& being cōſtrayned to carry
a burden one mile, goe two miles. And
with Paule the Apoſtle ſuffer falſe brethren & perſecutions, and bleſſe thoſe
who reuile and ſpeake ill of them.

The ſift degree of humility is, to manifeſt to his Abbot by humble confeſ-
ſion all the ill thoughts of his hart, and
ſecret faults committed by him. The
ſcripture exhorteth vs hereunto ſaying.
Reueale thy waye to our Lord, and
hope in him. And againe, Confeſſe to
our Lord becauſe he is good, becauſe
his mercy is for euer. And futhermore
the Prophet ſaith, I haue made knowne
vnto thee mine offence, & I haue not
hidden my iniuſtices. I haue ſaid, I will
declare openly againſt my ſelfe to our
Lord mine iuiuſtices : and thou haſt
pardoned the wickednes of my hart.

　　　　　　　　　　　　The

The sixt degree of humility is. If a monke be content with all basenes and extremity, & in all thinges which are inioyned him, he thinke himselfe an euill and vnworthy seruant, saying with the Prophet. I haue beene brought to nothing, & knew not. I haue beene made like a beast with thee, and I always with thee.

The seuenth degree of humility is, that he not onely pronounce with his tongue, but also with his very hart beleeue himselfe to be inferiour to all & most abiect; and humbling himselfe saye with the Prophet. I am a worme and not a man, the reproch of men & the outcast of the People. I am exalted, humbled and confounded. And againe, It is good for me that thou hast humbled me, that I may learne thy commandements.

The eight degree of humility is. That a monke doe nothing but what the common Rule of the monastery or the examples of his seniors teach and exhort him.

B 5   The

The ninght degree of humility is, For a monke to refraine his tongue frō speaking and be silent till a queſtion be asked him, remembring the saying of the scripture. In many words ſinne shall not be auoided;&that a talking man shall not be directed vpon earth.

The tenth degree of humility is, Not to be facile and prompt to laughter, for it is written, The foole exalteth his voice in laughter.

The eleuenth degree of humility is, For a monke when he ſpeaketh, to ſpeake gently and with out laughter, humbly, with grauity or fewe words, and diſcreetly, and not be clamorous in his voice; for it is written, A wise man is knowne by ſpeaking few words.

The twelfth degree of humility is For a monke not only to haue humility in his hart, but alſo to shew it in his exteriour to all that behold him ; at worke, in the Monaſtery, in the Oratorie, in the Garden, in the fielde, in the

the waye or wheresoeuer, sitting, walking or standing, that he haue alwayes
his head inclined & his eyes fixed on
the grownde, thinking himselfe euer
guilty for his sinnes, and ready to be
presented before the dreadfull iudge-
mēt of God, and so saying to himselfe
with the Publican of the Ghospell;
Lord, I a sinner am not worthy to lift
mine eyes vp to heauen. And againe
with the Prophet; I am bowed downe
and humbled on euery side. And
thus all these degrees of humility
being ascēded, a monke shall presently
come to that loue of God which is perfect and expelleth feare, whereby all
things which at the beginnig he obserued through feare, he shall now begin
to doe by custome without any labour
as it were naturally, not for the feare
of Hell, but for the loue of Christ, and
out of à good custome and a delight in
vertue, which our Lord will by the holy Ghost voutchsafe to worke in his
seruant now cleare from vice & sinne.

Of

Of the diuine office in the nightes.

C H A P. VIII.

IN the winter time, that is, from the kalends of Nouember till Easter according to à reasonable consideration, let them rise at the eight hower of the night, that they may rest till a little after midnight, and then after disgestion rise. As for the time that remaines after Mattines, let the Brethren who want some thing of the Psalter or lessons, bestowe it on meditation. But from Easter to the Kalends of Nouember, let the houre for Mattines soe be ordered, that a litle time being left for the Brethren to goe forth to the necessities of nature, by and by the Laudes which are to be said about the breake of daye may beginne.

How many Pſalmes are to be ſaide in the night howres.

Chap. IX.

IN winter time hauing firſt ſaid the verſe *Deus in adiutorium meum intende, Domine ad adiuuandum me feſtina,* then *Domine labia mea aperies & os meum annunciabit laudem tuam* is to be repeted thriſe. To which is to be added the third, Pſalme, & after it à *Gloria* Then the 94. Pſalme with an Anthym is to be ſayd or ſõge. Next after let a Hymne follow : and then ſix Pſalmes with Anthymes, which being ſaid with à verſe, let the Abbot giue bleſſing, Thẽ all ſitting doune on benches, let the brethren read three Leſſons by turnes, the booke lying on à trill, and after euery leſſon let à reſponſory be ſong. Let two reſponſaries be ſaid with out a *Gloria* : But after the third leſſon he who ſingeth it, let him alſo ſinge a *Gloria* which when the ſinger begineth

gineth let all rise from their seats, for
the honour & reuerence of the holy
Trinity. And let the scriptures as well
of the old testament as the new be
read at mattines, and the expositions
vpon them made by the most famous
orthodox & Cathoiik fathers. After
these three lessons & their responsories, let other six Psalmes follow, songe
with *alleluya.* After this let a lesson out
of the Apostle bee recited by hart,
and a verse & the supplication of the
Litanies that is a Kyrie eleyson,& soe
end the mattines or night Vigills.

*How the matines or night office is to bee
celebrated in summer.*

C H A P. X.

FRom Easter till the kalends of
Nouember, let the same number of
Psalmes be obserued as before we haue
appointed, but let not the Lessons be
read because of the shortnes of the
night, but in place of those three les-
                                    sons,

sons, let one be said by hart out of the old testament, & after that a short Responsory, and let the rest be performed as before is appointed, so that their neuer be fewer then twelue psalmes said at mattines, besides the third & 94. Psalme.

How the mattins or night office is to be celebrated on Sondayes.

Chap. XI.

ON the sundaye let them rise to mattines more timely, and obserue this order, that six Psalmes being song (as before we haue ordained) & the verse, let all sitt downe decently in their seats, each one in their order, let foure Lessons be read out of a Booke with their responsories, and in the fourth only let him that singes it saye the *Gloria*; at the beginning of which let all rise with reuerence. After these lessons, let six more Psalmes follow in order with their anthyms and a verse as before.

before. After which againe let ther
be read other foure lessons with their
responsories in the same order as the
former. And then let three canticles
be said out of the Prophets such as the
Abbot shall appoint which canticles
are to be songe with alleluya. Then the
verse being said & the Abbot hauing
giuen the benediction, let other foure
lessons be read out of the new testamēt
in the same orde as before, & after the
fourth responsory, let the Abbot beginne the Hymne *Te Deum laudamus*
which being said, let the Abbot read a
lesson of the Ghospell all standing with
reuerence and trembleing: which being
read; all answer Amen: and then let the
Abbot presently goe on with the
hymne *Te decet laus* : And the blessing
being giuen let him begin Laudes. This
order is alwayes to be obserued on
Sundayes in saying the vigills or mattines, as well in sommer as winter except perchance, (which God forbid it
happen) they ryse late, be cause then
some what is to be shortned of the
lessons

lessons or responsories. But let good heed be taken that this happen not and if it doe, let him by whose neglect it happeneth make satisfaction for it in the Oratory.

How the solemnity of Laudes is to be performed.

CHAP. XII.

FOr the sundaye Laudes, let first the sixt Psalme be said plaine without anthyme, after which saye the fiftieth Psalme with alleluya, and after that the hundred and seuenty Psalme and the sixty two Psalme. Then the Benedictions & praieres with à lesson out of the Apocalips by hart; and à responsory, à hymne and a verse with à canticle out of the Ghospell & the Litanies, and soe end.

How

*How the Laudes are to be celebrated on
priuat dayes.*

CHAP. XIII.

ON priuat dayes let laudes be thus
celebrated. Let the sixt Psalme be sayd with out an anthyme,
plaine and protracting it (as vpon sundaye) that all maye come to the fiftieth which is to be said with on Anthyme. After which let other two
Psalmes besayde according to the custome, that is on mundaye the fift and
fiue & thirtieth : on Tuesdaye the
forty two and the fiftieth six. On wed-
nesday the sixty third, and the sixtye
fourth. On Thurday the eighty seuen,
and the eighty ninth. On friday the
seuenty fiue & the ninty on : and on
saturday the hundreth and two, & the
canticle of Deuteronomie is to bee deuided in to two glorias. But on other
days let euery canticle, be said in his
day out of the Prophets according to
the

the practice of the church of Rome.
After these let the prayses or Laudate
follow, then a lesson without booke
out of the Apostle, a responsory, a
hymne, & a verse, a canticle out of the
Ghospell, the Litanies and soe end.
And let this allwayes be obserued, that
in the end of Laudes and Euen songe,
our Lords praier be said by the Prior a
loude that all maye heare it, for feare
of scandalls that ar wont to arise, but
being putt in mind by the couenant
of this praier, in which they saye, *for*
giue vs our trespasses as we for giue them
that trespasse against vs; they may purge
them selues of this vice. But in cele-
brating other howers, let only the last
part be said a loud, that all may answer.
Sed libera nos a malo.

In what maner mattines is to be celebrated
on the feast dayes of saints.

Chap. XIV.

VPon the feastes of saints and in
all solemnities, let the same order
be

be obſerned as vpon ſundays, only let
their be ſaid Pſalmes anthymnes and
leſſons pertayning to the day, but for
the reſt let the a foreſayd manner be
obſerued.

At what times Alleluya is to be ſaid.

CHAP. XV.

FRom the holy feaſt of Eaſter vntill
whitſontide with out intermiſſion
let alleluya be ſayd, as well with the
Pſalmes as the reſponſories. From
whitſontide till the begining of Lent
let it be ſayd at the Nocturnes with
the ſix laſt Pſalmes only. And vpon
euery ſonday out of Lent let the canticles of Laudes Prime, terce, ſext and
none be ſaid with alleluya, but Euen-
ſong with anthymes. And let the reſponſories neuer be ſayd with alleluya,
but only from Eaſter till whitſontide.

In

In what maner the worke of God or de-
uine seruice is to be performed in
the day tyme.

CHAP. XVI.

SEuen tymes adaye (saith the Prophet) I haue song praises to thee.
Which sacred number of seuen shall be
accomplished by vs. If at theses times,
of Laudes. Prime. Terce. Sext. None
Euensonge and Complin, we performe the office & duty of our seruice:
Be cause of these howers the Prophet
hath sayd, seuen tymes in the day. I
haue song praise to thee.   For of the
night vigills or mattins the selfe same
Prophet sayes. At midnight I did rise
to confesse to thee Therefore at these
tymes, let vs giue prayses to our sauiour, for the iudgements of his iustice.
That is at Laudes. Prime. Terce. Sext
none Euen songe & compline and in
the night let vs rise to confesse vnto
him.

How

How many Pſalmes ar to be ſaid at the
reſt of the howers.

C H A P. XVII.

VVE haue alredy ſet downe the
order of the office for the
Nocturnes and Laudes, now let vs diſpoſe of the howers following. At the
firſt hower or Prime let three Pſalmes
be ſaid ſeuerally, and not vnder one
gloria, ar.d a hymne of the ſame hower
preſently after the verſe *Deus in adiuto-*
rium meum intende , *Domine ad adiuuan-*
dum me feſtina , Before the Pſalmes.
And after the end of the Pſalmes, let
there be recited à leſſon, a verſe & ky-
rye eleyſon, and let them haue licence
to departe. Terce Sext ād :None are to
be recited after the ſame order : that is
a verſe and a hymne, at the ſame hower
three Pſalmes, then a leſſon, a verſe, and
kyrie eleyſon, and after that leaue to
depart. If the conuent be great let them
be ſonge with anthymes if litle, only
recited.

ꝶecited. But let euenſonge be ſaide
with foure Pſalmes and anthymnes
after which Pſalmes let a leſſon be recited then à reſpóſory, a hymne, a verſe
a canticle out of the ghoſpel the lita-
nie and our Lords praier ſo end. For
complin let there be three Pſalmes recited plaine with out anthymes, after
which, a hymne fitt for that hower, a
Leſſon, a verſe, kyrie eleyſon and a Benediction, and ſo make an end.

*In what order the Pſalmes are to
be ſaid.*

Chap. XVIII.

IN the daye howers firſt of all let
them alwayes begin with the verſe,
*Deus in adiutorium meum intende, Domi-
ne ad adiuuandum me feſtina* and a *Gloria,*
then the hymne of that howre. At
prime on ſondayes there are to be ſaid
fower Chapters of the hundred and
eighteenth Pſalme. And at the reſt of
the howers to witt, Terce Sext and
None

None let there be sayd three chapters of the same hundred and eightieth Psalme. Prime on mondaye let there be said three Psalmes, that is the first seconde and sixth, and soe euery daye at Prime till sondaye let three Psalmes be said in order vnto the ninetieth Psalme, but soe that the nineth and seuenth Psalme be diuided in to two Glorias; And soe it will fall out that on the sunday at mattines we shall allwayes begin from the twentyeth Psalme. At Terce Sext & none of the sundayes let the nine chapters which remayne of the one hundred and eightieth Psalme be said by three & three at the some howres. The hundred and eightieth Psalme therefore being said ouer in two days, to witt sunday and mondaye; At Terce, Sext and none vpon Tuesday let the Psalmes be sung in order by three & three from the hundredth and ninetieth to the hundredth twenty seuenth, that is, nine Psalmes. And these Psalmes ar allways to be repeated at the some howers the rest of the week

week till sunday ; An vniforme order also of the hymnes, Lessons, and verses, being euery day obserued ; soe they maye all euery sundaye begin from the hundred and eighteen Psalme.

Euen song is euery daye to be songe with foure Psalmes, which Psalmes are to begin from the hundredth & ninth Psalme going on to the hundredth fourty seuenth, excepting only such, as ar sequestred for other howres , that is from the hundred and seuent ten Psalme to the hundred twenty and seauen, and the hundred thirty three, & the hundred forty two. All the rest ar to be said in euensonges. And be cause there fall three Psalmes short, those Psalmes which ar found longest ar to be diuided , that is the hundred thirty eight , the hundred forty three and the hundred fourty fowre; And let the hūdreth and sixteenth because it is short be ioyned with the hundredth and fifteenth. The order therfore of the Psalmes for euensonge being set downe, let the other things that is les-

sons

fons, Refponfories, hymes, verfes, and
Canticles be ordered as we haue faid
before.   At complin let the fame
Pfalme be repeated euery daye, that is
the fourth, nintieth, and the hundred
thirty three.

The order of the day office being
thus difpofed, let all the Pfalmes which
remayne be equally deuided into the
feuen Mattines or night Vigills, deui-
ding ftill the Pfalmes which ar longeft:
And let twelue be appointed for euery
night. And if this difpofition and diftri-
bution of the Pfalmes difpleafe any, let
him if he think good order them otherwife, fo he prouide that euery weeke
the whole Pfalter of a hundred and
fifty Pfalmes be fonge; And that vpon
funday at Mattines they begin it a-
gaine. Be caufe Monkes shew them
felues ouer negligent & indeuout, if in
the circuit of a weeke, they finge not
ouer the Pfalter with the accuftomed
canticles, fince wee read that our holy
fathers haue couragioufly performed
all that in one daye, which God grant
                                    we

we tepid and negligent persons maye
performe in a whole weeke.

*Of the order and discipline of
singinge.*

Chap. XIX.

VVE beleeue the diuine presence to be in all places, and
the eyes of our Lord continually to behold both the good & the bad: But
then especially and particularly , when
we ar at the worke of God. Therfore
let vs be allways mindfull what the
Prophet saith: *Serue yee our Lord in feare*
and againe; *Singe yee wisely,* and *In the
sight of Angells I will sing vnto thee.*
Therfore let vs consider in what maner, and with what reuerence it behoueth vs to be in the sight of God and
the Angells, and let vs soe sing in the
quire that our mind and voyce accord together.

C 2   *Of*

Of the reuerence of prayer.

CHAP. XX.

IF wee presume not to speake with any great perso̅, but with humility & reuerance, how much more ought wee to present our supplications to our Lord the God of all thinges with humility and purity of deuotion. And we must know that we shall be heard, not for our many words, but for our purity of hart, and compunction of teares. And therefore prayer ought to be short & pure, vnlesse perhaps it be prolonged by the inspiration of diuine grace. But in the conuent let praier always be short; and the signe being giuen by the Priour, let all rise to-geather.

Of the

*Of the Deanes of the Monaſ-
tery.*

CHAP. XXI.

IF the Conuent be great, let their
be choſen out of them ſome Brothers who ar of good repute and holy conuerſation, & appointed Deanes,
who ar to be carefull ouer their dean-
ries in all things according to the com-
mandement of God, and the precepts
of their Abbot. And let ſuch men be
choſen for Deanes, whom the Abbot may ſecurely rely on to bear part
of his burden. And let them not be
choſen by order, but according to
their deſert of life and learning. And
if perhaps any of them puft vp with
pride, ſhall be found worthy of re-
prehenſion, and being rebuked once
twice or thrice doe not amend, let him
be put out of office, and an other
who is worthy, ſubſtituted in his place. And the ſame we ordain of the
Prior or Prepoſitus.

C 3　　　　*How*

How the Monkes ar to sleepe.

Chap. XXII.

LEt the Monkes sleepe a part in seuerall Beds, and let them haue bedclothes befitting them according to the appointment of the Abbot. If it can be, let them sleepe in one place. But if the number permit it not, let thē sleepe by tenne or twenty in a place with their seuerall seniors who haue care of them. And let a candel burne In the same cell till morning. Let them sleepe clothed and girt with girdells or cordes, but let them not haue kniues by their sides while they sleepe, lest perhaps they be hurt there with sleeping. And let the Monkes be allwayes ready, that as soon as the signe is heard, rising speedely each one may hasten to come before his fellowes to the worke of God, yet with all grauity and modestie. Let not the yonger brethren

thren haue beds by themſelues , but
mixt with the elder : and ryſing let thē
modeſtly exhort one another to the
worke of God ; for the excuſes and de-
layes of ſuch as be ſluggiſh.

Of excommunication for of-
fences.

C H A P. XXIII.

IF any brother ſhall be found ſtubborne, diſſobedient, proud, murmuring, or contrarie in any thinge to the
holy Rule , or to contemne the orders
of his ſeniours, let that man according
to the precept of our Lord be once or
twiſe ſecretly admoniſhed by his ſeniours, and if he doe not amende, let
him be reprehended publikely before
all , but if with all th s he amend not,
then let him be lyable to excommunication, if he vnderſtand what kinde of
puniſhment it is. And if he be obſtinat,
let him be lyable to corporall puniſhment.

C 4 *What*

What the manner of excommunication
ought to be.

CHAP. XXIV.

According to the quality of the
falt, the meafure of excōmunication or punishment ought to be extended; which is to depend on the iudgement of the Abbot. If any brother be
found in a leffer falt, let him be depriued of the participation of the table : The manner of this depriuation
shall be this : that in the oratorie he
shall neyther beginne Pfalme, nor anthyme, nor recite a leffon vntill he
haue made fatisfaction. And let him
take his refection of meate alone after
the brethren haue taken their refectiō
in fuch meafure, and at fuch time as
his Abbot shall thinke fitting; as (for
example) if the brethren take their refection at the fixt hower, let that
brother at the ninth : if the brethren
at the ninth, let him at the euening,
                                    vntill

vntill by dew satisfaction he obtaine
pardon.

Of more greeuous faults.

Chap. XXV.

BVt that brother who is guilty of
more greeuious faults, is to bee suf-
pended both from the table and the o-
ratorie. And let none of the brethren
difcourfe with him or keepe him cō-
pany, let him be alone at the worke
inioyned him perfifting in penance &
forrow, knowing that terrible fen-
tence of the Apoftle, who fayeth that
fuch à man is deliuered to fathan to
the diftruction of the flesh, that his
fpirit maye bee faued in the daye of
our Lord. And let him take his allowance of meate alone in fuch meafure
and time, as the Abbot fhall thinke fitt,
neyther let any man bleffe h'm paffing
by, or the meate which is giuen him.

Of those that keepe company with ex-
communicated persons without
the commande of the
Abbot.

Chap. XXVI.

IF any brother shall presume without cōmand of the Abbot to ioyne
himselfe in any sort to an excommunicated brother, or to talke with him,
or send to him , let him incurre the
same penalty of excomunication.

How the Abbot ought to be carefull of
such as be excommunicated.

Chap. XXVII.

LEt the Abbot haue a speciall care
of the delinquent brethren, for the
Phisitian is not needfull for such as ar
in health, but for the sicke. And therfore he ought to vse all the means of a
wise Phisitian, and to send to them
some

some priuat comforters. That is some
antient and discreet bethren, who may
as it weare secretly comfort the troobled brother, & stirr him vp to hūble
satisfaction. And let them comfort
him, that he be not opressed with ouer
much sorrow but as the Apostle saith;
let charity be confirmed in him and let
all praye for him. The Abbot ought
to be very solicitous and carefull with
all prudence and industrie, that he
loose none of the sheepe committed to
his charg. Let him know that he hath
vndertakē the charge of infirme soules,
& not any tyranicall autority ouer
such as be well. And let him feare the
threatnings of the Prophet, by whom
God saith: what yee sawe well liking
that you take to your selues, & what
was weake you threw away. Let him
imitate the pious example of the good
shepheard, who leauing ninety nine
sheepe in the mountaynes, went to
seeke one sheepe which was gone af-
traye, on whose infirmity he tooke
such compassion, that he vouchsafed

to

to lay it on his shoulders and so to cary it backe to the flocke.

Of those who being often corrected
do not amend.

Chap. XXVIII.

IF à brother haue beene often admonished of a fault, or beene excommunicated and yet do not amend, let him be more seuerely corrected, and punished with stripes. And if for all this he amend not, so but rather puffed vp with pride (which God for bid) will also defend his doings, then let the Abbot doe like a wise Phisitian, after that he hath applied the fomentations, and oyntments of good exhortations, the medicines of diuine scripture, and last of all the punishment of excommunication, and the stripes of Rods, and yet find his labours take not effect, let him add that which is more then all this to witt his prayer, and the prayers of all the Brethren for him,

that

that our Lord who can doe all thinges,
would vouchsafe to work a cure vpon
the infirme brother : and if by this
meanes he be not healed and amended,
then let the Abbot vse the sword of ab-
scission according to the saying of the
Apostle : Take away euill from a-
mongst you. And againe. If the vn-
faithfull breaking his promise depart,
let him depart, least one diseased sheepe
infect the whole flocke.

Whether brethren gonne out of the Monas-
tery ought to be receaued
againe.

CHAP. XXIX.

THat brother who through his
owne fault goeth forth, or is cast
forth of the monastery, if he will returne, let him promise first the amen-
dement of the fault for which he went
forth, and then let him be receaued in
the lowest rank, that by this, his humility may be tried. And if he goe out a-
gaine

gaine let him be receaued againe till
the thirdtime. But afterwards let him
know that all entrance will be denied
him.

*Of Children of yonger yeares how thy ar
to be corrected.*

C H A P. XXX.

EVery age & vnderstanding ought
to haue a proper gouerment. And
therefore as often as children, or such
as are younger in age & can not vnderstand how great a punishment excommunication is, let such as these when
they offend be punished with rigorous
fasting or sharpe stripes, that so they
be cured.

*What kind of man the Cellerarius of the
Monastery ought to be.*

C H A P. XXXI.

LEt such à one be chosen out of the
conuent to be Cellerarius of the
Monastery, who is wise, graue of be-
hauiour

hauiour, sober, noe greet eater, not
turbulent, not iniurious, not slow or negligent, nor prodigall, but one that fea-
reth God, who maye be as a father to
all the conuent : let him haue care of
all things, and let him doe nothing
without the command of his Abbot.
Let him obserue such things as ar commanded him, and let him not contristate his brethren. And if any brother
request any thing of him that is not reasonable, let him not contristate him
by contemning him, but let him with
humility and iust cause deny his vnrea-
sonnable request : let him haue regard
to his owne soule, and be mindfull of
that rule of the Apostle: That he which
serueth well getteth him selfe a place
amongst the iust. Let him haue a diligent care of the sicke, of the infants, of
the guestes, and of the poore, for of all
these let him know at the dredfull iudgement daye, he is to giue an accompt;
keep & regard all the vessells & goods
of the Monastery, as if they were sacred vessells of the alter, let nothing be
neglected neuer. Let him neither be
                              couetuous

couetous nore prodigall or a waſter
of the goods of the Monaſtery. But let
him doe all things with moderation,
and according to the command of the
Abbot, aboue all things let him ſeek,
to conſerue humility, and if any thing
be asked of him which he hath not to
giue, let him at the leaſt afford them a
good anſwere, for it is written, a good
anſwer is before the beſt gueſt; Let him
haue à care of all thinges which the
Abbot inioyneth him, and let him not
preſume to doe any thing which he
forbiddeth. Let him giue to the brethren their allowance of meat appointed, with out leſſening or delayeing it,
that they be not ſcandalized, being
mindfull of our Lord ſayings in the
Ghoſpell, what he deſerueth that shall
ſcandalize one of the litle ones. It the
conuent be great, let aſſiſtance begiuē
him that ſoe being holpen he may
quietly performe the office committed
to his charge. Let ſuch thinges as are to
be giuen or asked, be giuen & asked
at conuenient houres, that noe man
                                    maye

maye be troubled or contristated in
the house of God.

Of the Iron tooles of the Monas-
tery.

CHAP. XXXII.

FOr keeping the Iron tooles,
Clothes, or other things belonging
to the Monastery, let the Abbot prouide brethren of whose life and conuersation he maye be secure, and to them
let him allot all things to be keept, as
he shall iudge most expedient. Of all
which thinges let the Abbot keepe à
note, that when other brethren succed,
the one may know what he takes, and
the other wh t he quiteth, and if any
one shall sluttishly or negligently
handle the things of the monastery,
let him be rebuked. And if hedoe not
amend, let him be lyable to discipline.

Whether

*Whether the monkes ought to haue any
thinges proper to them-
selues.*

CHAP. XXXIII.

THe vice of giuing or taking
without the leaue of the Abbot, or
calling of any thing whatsoeuer, euen
of a booke or pen his owne is especially
to be rooted out of the monastery. Because it is not lawfull for them to haue
their bodies or wills in their owne power. But to hope for all necessaryes
from the father of the monastery. Nothing which the Abbot doth not giue
or permitt may be lawfally keept but
all things to be in common, as it is
written. Nor lett any call or presume
any thinge to be his owne. And if any
one shall be founde to be giuen to this
most wicked vice, let him be admonished once or twice, & if he shall not
amend, let him be subiect to correction.

Whether

*Whether all ought to haue necessaries
alike.*

Chap. XXXIV.

AS it is written, let there be di-
stributed to each one according
to their necessity ; to signify , not that
there shall be acception of persones
(which god forbid) but that consideration be had of euery ones infirmities.
And therfore let him who needeth
lesse , giue God thankes , and not be
contristated. And he who needeth
more , let him be humbled for his infirmity & not proude for the mercy
shewed him, and soe all the members
shall be in peace. Aboue all thinges
take heed there be noe murmuration
vpon any occasion what so euer by
word or signe , and if any one shall be
founde falty in this , let him be liable
to most seuere discipline.

Of

*Of the weekly officers which are to be in
the kitchin.*

Chap. XXXV.

THe brethren are soe to serue each
other, that noe man be excused
from the office of the kitchin, vnlesse
they be hindred by sicknes or other
busines of more profitt. Becaufe from
thence a greater reward is gotten. And
for the weaker fort, let them haue help
that they may doe it wich alacrity and
not with fadnes; and let all generally
haue help and folace according as the
number of the conuent and fituatiõ of
the place shall require. If the conuent
be great let the Cellerarius be excufed
from the kitchin, & as we haue faid
before, such as ar imployed in matters
of greater profit But let the reft ferue
each other in charity. He who goeth
out of the weeke, let him vpon faturday
make all things cleane. Let him
wash the linen with which the bre-

                                            thren

thren wipe their hands & feet. And let
both him who goeth out, & he who
cometh in, wash the feet of euery one.
And let him giue back by tale to the
Cellerarius the veſſels of his office
made cleane and whole, that he maye
know what he giueth & what he
taketh.

And theſe weeke officiers maye
take an hower before refection, eache
one a draught of drink, and a peece of
bread a boue the appointed allowance,
that at the houer of refection, they
maye ſerue their brethren with out
murmuring or great labour. Not with-
ſanding on ſolemne days, let all for-
beare till mas. The weeke officers en-
tring in, & going out, vpon ſondaye in
the oratory, preſently after Laudes,
ſhall make low inclination at the feet
of their brethren, & deſier to be prayed
for. And Theye who goeth out that
weeke, ſhall ſaye this verye. *Benedi-*
Etus es Domine Deus, qui adiuuiſti me &
conſolatus es me. which being thrice repeated let him who goeth out receaue
his

his blessing, and let him who entreth immediatly follow & saye *Deus in adiutorium meum intende*, *Domine ad adiuuandum me festina*, and let this be likwise thrice repeated of all. And hauing receaued his blessing, let him enter in to his office.

Of the sicke brethren.

CHAP. XXXVI.

BEfore and aboue all things a speciall care is to be had of the sicke, so that they be serued, euen as Christ himselfe because he hath sayd; I haue beene sicke & yee haue visited me. And what yee haue donne to one of these litle ones, yee haue donne to me. let the sicke brethren consider that they are serued for the honour of God, & therfore let them not contristat their brethren who serue them, with their superfluityes. Who notwitstanding ar patiently to be borne with all, because of such, a more aboundant reward is gotten.

gotten. Therefore let the Abbot haue
a speciall care they be not neglected.
For the sick brethren let their be a cell
appointed by it selfe, & a seruitor fearing God, that is diligent & carefull.
Let the vse of bathes be allowed to the
sicke as often as shall be expedient: but
to such as are in health especially to
yonge men, let it bee seldome granted.
More ouer let eating of flesh be granted to such as are sicke, & weake, for
their recouery. But when they ar recouered let them after the acustomed
manner, wholy abstaine from flesh.
And let the Abbot baue a speciall care,
that the Cellerarius or seruitors neglect
not the sicke, be cause whatsoeuer is
donne amisse by his disciples, is imputed to him.

Of old men & Infants.

Chap. XXXVII.

ALthough mans nature it selfe
be inclined to pitty, these ages,
that is,

that is, old men & Infants, not withstanding it is also fitting that by the autority of the Rule they should be prouided for. Let therefore their weaknes
be all ways considered, & let the ri-
gour of the Rule in victualls be by noe
means kept with them, but let there
be a pious consideration had of them,
and let them come timely to the canonicall howers.

Of the weekely reader.

CHAP. XXXVIII.

REeadinge ought not to be wanting at the Table whiles the brethren eate ; Neither ought any one to
presume to reade , who shall take vp,
the booke by hap hazard , but let him
that is appointed to read for the whole
weeke enter in vpon sondaye. And
then after masse and communion let
him desier all to praye for him , that
God may keep from him the spirit of
pride, and let this verse be thrise repeated

ted in the oratory, he first begining it.
Domine labia mea aperies, & os meum a-
nuntiabit laudem tuam. Then after the
benediction giuen, let him enter in to
reade. Let great silence be kept at the
table, soe that noe voyce or muttering
be hard, but only of the reader, and for
such thinges as ar necessary for meate
& drinke, let the brethren soe prouide,
that no man neede to aske any thing.
And if any thing shall be wanting, let
it be asked rather by the sound of some
signe then by voyce: nor let any one
there presume to aske any thing of
that which is read, or any thinge else,
least occasion of speech be giuen, vnlesse perhaps the Prior will make some
breefe exhortation for the edification
of the brethren. And let the hebdoma-
darius take a few pottage before he beginne to reade, for holy communion
sake, and least perhaps it be troublesome to him to fast soe long & afterwards let him eate with the other
weekely officers of the kitchim and
seruitours. And let not the brethren

D   singe

or reade by order, but such as maye edifie the hearers.

*Of the measure or quantity
of meate.*

CHAP. XXXIX.

AT the dayly refection as well of the sixth as ninth hower at all tables, we thinke two dishes of hot pulse will be fitting, by reason of the infirmyties of diuers, that he who can not eate of one, may make his refection of the other. Let therefore two dishes of hot pulse suffice the brethren, and if there bee any apples or frute, let them haue it for a third dish. Let à pound of bread be the allowance for one daye, whether ther be one refection, or both dinner and supper, and if they be to suppe, let a third part of that pound be reserued by the Cellerarius for their supper. And if their labour be great, it shall be in the power of the Abbot to add to their ordinary allowance what

he

he shall thinke expedient, hauing alwayes a care to auoid excesse and surfi-
ting, that the monkes be not ouertak-
en with indisgestion, be cause there is
noe sinne more contrary to à christian
then gluttonie, and our Lord saith; see
that your harts be not opprest with
gluttonie & drunckennes. But to children of yonger age, let not the same
quantity be giuen, but lesse then to the
elder; obseruing alwayes moderation
and frugality. And lett all generally
abstayne from eating of foure footed
beasts, excepting such as be very weake
and sick.

Of the measure of drinke.

CHAP. XXXX.

EVery one hath his proper gift
from God one thus & another
thus: and therfore we appoint the measure of other mens victualls not with
out some scrupulosity. Yet considering the weaknes & infirmity of

many, wee thinke a pinte of wine will suffice each one a daye. But to whom God giues the giuft of abstinence, let them know they shall receaue their proper reward. And if either labour, heate of the sommer, or situation of the place require more, let the Prior doe what he thinketh good, hauing euer a care that fullnes or gluttony creepe not in. And although we reade, wine to be in no sort the drink of Monckes, yet because in these times they will not be so perswaded, let vs at-leastwise cōsent to this, that we drinke not our fill but sparingly & with moderation, because wine makes euen wisemen to Apostatike. But where the necessity of the place will not allowe that measure appointed, but lesse or perhaps none at all, let them prayse God that liue there, & not murmur. And this aboue all things we admonish, that there neuer be any murmurations.

At

At what howers the brethren ar to take
their refection.

Chap. XXXXI.

FRom the holy feaſt of Eaſter vntill
whitſontide, let the brethren take
their refeƈtion at the ſixt hower , &
ſuppe at night. But from whitſontide
all the ſummer longe , if they labour
not in the feilds, or the extremity of
the heate doth not moleſt them , let
them faſt wedenſday & friday till the
ninth hower, but on other days, let
them dine at the ſixth hower: Which
ſixth hower of dinner if they worke in
the feilds or the heate of the ſommer be
great, ſhall be continued, at the diſcretion of the Abbot, and let him ſoe temper & diſpoſe all things, that ſoules may
be ſaued and what the brethren doe,
maye be done without murmuring.
But from the Ides of ſeptember vntill
the beginning of Lent, let the brethrē
always refreſh themſelues at the ninth
D 3   hower:

hower; And from the beginning of
Lent vntill Eafter, let them refresh in
the euening, but let it be foe ordered,
that then in the euening there be noe
need of à light at time of refection, but
that all be done by daye light, yea at
all times whether fupper or noe fupper,
let the hower of refection be foe ordered, that all things be donne by day-
light.

*That noe man maye fpeake after
Complin.*

Chap.   XXXXII.

Monkes ought to keep filence at
all times but efpecially in the
night howers. And therefore at all
times, whether they be dayes of fafting
or dining, when it is a day of dining,
prefently after they are rifen from
fupper, let them come all together, and
being fett, let one reade the collations
or liues of the fathers, or fome other
thing that maye edifie the hearers, but
let

let them not reade the Heptateuch or
booke of kings, be cause it will not be
profitable for weake vnderstandings
to heare this scripture at that hower,
yet at other times it may be read. But
if it be a fasting daye after that Euen-
fonge is saide, with in a litle space let
them come to the reading of the Collations as we haue sayd : and foure or
fiue leaues beeing read, or as much as
the time permits, all being come together in this time of reading and namely
those who perhaps were occupyed in
some speciall workes enioyned them
when all ar assembled together, let
them say Complin, and after they
goe out from Complin, let noe leaue
be granted to speake that night. And if
any one shall be found to breake this
Rule of silence, let him be liable to
most seuere punishment, except there
be some necessary occasion by reason
of the coming in of some guests, or that
the Abbot commande any thing, And
let that also be donne with great grauity & moderation.

Of

*Of those that comes late to the works of
God, or to the Table.*

Chap. XXXXIII,

LEt all come presently as-soone as
the signe shall be giuen with all
hast to the diuine office, leauing whatsoeuer shall be in their hands. Yet
with grauity and auoiding all kind of
scurillity , let nothing therefore be
preferred before the worke of God.
And if any shall come to the Mattines
after the gloria of the 94. Psalme
(which of purpose we will haue to
be said with protraction and leasurly)
let him not stande in his order in the
quire, but let him stand last of all, or
in the place which the Abbot shall ap-
pointe à parte, for such negligent
People, that he maye be in the sight
of the Abbot and all the rest , vntill
the worke of God be ended , that so
he doe penance & make publik satisfaction; And we ordaine that they stād
in

in the laſt place , or apart, to the end
that being ſeen by all, they may amend
euen for ſhame. For it maye be ſuch a
one who if he remayne out of the oratorie, wil perhaps ſetle himſelfe to
ſleepe or idle talke, & ſoe giue occaſiõ
to the enimy. Therefore let him come
in, that he looſe not all, and bee amended for the time to come.

And in the daye howers, he that
shall come to the worke of God after
the verſe & gloria, of the firſt Pſalme,
according to the afore ſayd order , let
him ſtand laſt , and let him not preſume to aſſociate himſelfe to the quiet
of the ſingers, vntill he haue made ſatisfaction, except the Abbot shall giue
leaue by his permiſſion , yet ſoe, that
afterwards he make ſatisfaction. And
to the hower of refection , he that cometh not before the verſe,ſoe that they
may ſay the verſe and praye all together and ſitt downe together at the table,he I ſaye that through negligence
shal offende in this,let him be rebuked
vntill the ſeconde time. If after he doe

not amend, let him not be admitted to the participation of the common table : But being sequestred from the company of his brethren, let him eate a lone, & his portion of wine be taken from him till satisfaction and amendment. And let him in like manner suffer , who is not present at that verse which is said after meate. Nor let any man presume to take any meat or drinke, before the appointed hower, or after it. Moreouer if any thinge be offered to any one by the Prior and he refuse it, at the time he shall desier , let him not receaue that or any thinge else vntill he haue made sufficient satisfaction.

Of those that are excommunicated how they maye satisfie.

CHAP. XXXXIV.

HE who is excommunicated from the oratorie or table for more greeuous offences , at the hower in
which

which the worke of God is celebrated
in the oratorie, let him lye proſtrat before the doores of the oratorie ſaying
nothing, but lying his head on the
ground, proſtrat all along at the feet of
all thoſe that goe out of the oratorie.
And let him doe this ſoe longe, till the
Abbot think he hath made ſufficient
ſatisfaction : Who being commanded
to come to the Abbot, shall caſt himſelfe at his feet, and afterward at the
feet of all his brethren, that they maye
pray for him. And then if the Abbot
shall commande, let him be receued in
to the quire, and in the ranke which
the Abbot shall oppointe, yet ſoe, that
he preſume not to beginne a Pſalme, or
Leſſon, or any thing elſe in the oratorie, vnleſſe the Abbot againe commande. And at all howers when the
worke of God is finished, let him caſt
himſelfe on the earth in the place where
he ſtands, and let him ſatisfie in this
manner vntill the Abbot command
him to ceaſe, from this ſatisfaction. But
they who for litle faults ar excomuni-
                                    cated,

cated, only from the table, let them satisfy in the oratory as longe as the Abbot commandeth: And let them doe this, vntill he blesse them and saye, it sufficeth.

Of those who committ any error in the Oratorie.

CHAP. XXXXV.

IF any one while he reciteh à Psalme, responsorie, antiphone, or Lesson, shall erre, and maketh not humble satisfaction there before all, let him be liable to greater punishment, as one that will not amend with humility, what by negligence he hath donne à misse, and let children be beaten for such a fault.

Of

Of those who offend in lesser matters.

Chap. XXXXVI.

IF any one whilest he is in labour eyther in the kitchin, cellar, or any office, in the bakehouse, garden, or in any art, shall doe any thinge a misse or breake or loose any thinge, or shall committ any excesse, and doe not presently come before the Abbot or conuent, and of his owne accord satisfie and confesse his offence; when it shall be knowne by another, let him be liable to greater punishment. But if it shall be priuat to his owne soule, as being a sinne, let him only manifest it to his Abbot or spirituall seniours, who knowe how to cure their owne wounds, and not to disclosse or publish an other mans.

Of

Of appointing the hower of diuine
seruice.

C H A P. XXXXVII.

LEt it be the Abbots care night and
daye to signifie the hower of the
worke of God, eyther by himselfe, or
committing the care there of to some
vigilant brother to see that all thinges
be done in competent howers. And let
them who ar appointed , beginne
Psalmes and antiphones each one in
their order after the Abbot. And let not
any presume to singe or reade, but he
that can so performe the office, that the
hearers may be edified by it. Which
ought to be done with humility, grauity, & trembling, and by him whom
the Abbot shal appoint.

Of the dayly hand labour.

C H A P.   XXXXVIII.

IDlenes is an enemy of the soule,
and therefore at certaine howers the
brethren

brethren ought to be imployed in han-
dye labour, and other whiles in spirituall reading. And therefore we thinke
that both times may ethus be well ordered : that is, from Easter vntill the
kalends of october, in the morning
going out from Prime, they doe that
which shall be necessary vntill well
nigh the fourth hower. And from the
fourth hower till well nigh the sixt
hower, let them be imployed in reading, & after the sixt hower rising frō
table, let them rest on their Beds with
all silence, and he who then perhaps
desires to reade, let him reade soe to
him selfe, that he disquiet not other.
Let None be said some that sooner,
about the eight houre, and after that
let them doe what they haue to doe
vntill euening. And if the necessity of
the place, or pouerty require that they
themselues be imployed in reaping
their corne, let them not be contristated. Because they are then truly
Monkes when they liue by the labour
of their hands, as both our fathers and
the

the Apoſtles did. Yet let all thinges be
done in meaſure by reaſon of ſuch as
are puſillanimous.

And from the kalends of october
vntill the beginning of Lent, let them
be imployed in reading till full the ſecond hower, and at the ſecond hower,
let Terce be celebrated, then vntill the
ninth hower, let all labour in the
worke which is enioyned them. But
the firſt ſigne of the ninth hower being
giuen, let them all departe from theire
worke, and let them be ready when
the ſecond ſigne shall be made. And
after refection let them be imployed
in reading of ſpirituall bookes or
Pſalmes.

But in Lent let them be imployed
in readinge from the morninge till the
third howre compleat : and vntill the
tenth hower compleat let them doe
the worke enioyned them. In whih
time of Lent, let each one take à booke
out of the Librarie, reade it all ouer in
order ; and let theſe bookes be giuen
them in the begining of Lent. Let

[there

there be diligent care taken, that there be one or two feniors appointed, who maye goe vp and downe the Monaftery at the howers in which the brethrē ar imployed in reading, to fee leaft any of them be flouth full, or applie himfelfe to idlenes or foulish talke, and ne- glecte his reading, and foe not only vn- profitable to himfelfe, but alfo an im- pedimēt to others. If fuch a one (which god forbid) be founde, let him be re- prehended once or twice, and if he a- mend not, let him be liable to regular difcipline, foe that others maye take warning by it. Neither let one brother affociat himfelf which an other at in- competent howers. On fondaye let all be imployed in reading, except fuch as are deputed for officers. And if any one shall be fo flouthfull or negligent, that he will not or cannot meditate or read, let him haue fome worke inioy- ned him to keepe him from idlenes. To the weake brethren, & tender of con- ftitution, let fuch worke or art be inioy- ned as they maye be kept from idlenes,
and

and yet not oppressed with soe much
labour so as to be driuen awaye, whose
weaknes therefore ought to be well
considered by the Abbot.

Of the obseruance of Lent.

C H A P.   XXXXIX.

ALthough at all tymes the life of
à Monke ought to be as à continuall Lent, yet because fewe are soe
vertuous, we therfore exhort them at
least in this holy time of Lent, to lead
their life in all purity and to wash a-
waye all the negligences of other
times. Which then we shal righly performe, if we refraine from all vices,
and apply our selfes to praier with weeping, to reading, compunction of hart
and abstinence. Therefore in these
dayes, let vs add some thinge ouer &
aboue our wonted taske, peculiar
prayers, and abstinence from meat &
drincke, so that euery one aboue the
ordinary measure appointed him, of his
 owne

owne free will, with ioye of the holy
ghofte offer fome thinge to God: That
is, that he withdraw from his body
fome what of his meat, drinke, fleepe,
talke, laughter, and with fpirituall
ioye & defire, expect the holy Eafter.
Yet let euery one make his Abbot ac-
quainted with this very thinge which
he offers, and let it be done with his
praier & confent. Becaufe whatfoeuer
is done whitout the permiffion of the
fpirituall father, shall be imputed to
prefumption and vaine glorie, and me-
riteth note rewarde. All thinges therefore are to be done with the leaue and
permiftion of the Abbot.

Of brethren who labour farr from
the oratorie, or fuch as ar on
the waye.

Chap. L.

THe brethren who ar in labour very farr of, and cannot come in a
competent houre to the oratorie, and
the

the Abbot knowes it is foe, let them
there doe the worke of God, where
they labour, kneeling with feare & reuerence. And let thē alfo who ar fent
à iourney, haue care not to flip the appointed howers, but doe as they can,
and by no meanes neglect to performe their taske of diuine feruice.

Of Brethren who goe not far of.

Chap. LI.

THe Brethren who goe forth vpō
any errand and hope to returne
that daye to the Monaftery , let them
not prefume to eate abroad , although
they be intreated, vnleffe their Abbot
command them. And if they doe otherwife, let them be excommunicated.

*Of the oratorie of the Monaf-
terie.*

Chap. LII.

LEt the oratorie be that which the
name fignifieth, and let not any o-
ther

ther thinge be done or wrought there; The worke of God being ended, let all goe forth with exceding great silence making reuerence to God, that the Brother who perhaps will peculiarly pray by himselfe, be not hindred by the lewdnes of an other. And if another will also praye priuatly by himselfe, let him simply enter, and praye, not in a clamorous voice, but with teares and attention of hart. Therefore let not any who doth not pray, be permitted to staye in the oratorie after the worke of God be finished, leaft he be a hinderance to others.

Of the manner of entertayninge Gueftes.

Chap. LIII.

LEt all guefts that comme to the Monaftery be entertayned like Chrift : becaufe he will fay : I haue been a gueft and yee haue entertained me. And let due honour be giuen to
all,

all, especially to those of the houshold of faith and trauellers. Assoone therefore as à guest is come, let the Prior meet him or the brethren with all shew of charity; and let them first pray together, & soe be associated to each other in peace. And let not the kisse of peace be offered, but after prayer, by reason of the illusions of the deuill. And in the salutation it selfe, let all humility be shewed. The head beinge bowed downe or all the body prostrate on the earth to all guests comming and goeing, let Christ who is receaued in them be adored in them. Let the guests receaued be brought to prayer, and afterwards let the Prior or whosoeuer he shall command sitt, and keep company with them. Let the diuine law be read before the guest that he maye be edified, and afterwards let all courtesie be shewed to him. Let à regular fast be broke by the Prior for the entertainment of à guest: vnlesse it be a principall day of fast, which ought not to be broken. But let the

brethren

hold on their custome of fasting. Let
the Abbot giue water to the guests
hands, and let both the Abbot and the
whole conuent wash the feet of the
guests, which being done let them
saye this verse, *suscepimus Deus miseri-*
cordiam tuam in medio templi tui. And
let poore people and strangers especially be diligently entertayned with
all care, because in the Christ is more
truly receaued. For the feare or terrour
of rich men doth it self exhort an honour to them.

Let the kitchin of the Abbot and
guest be apart, that guest without whō
the Monastery neuer is, comming at
vncertaine howers, may not disquiet
the Brethren. Into which kitchin let
then enter two brothers for a yeare
who can well performe that office. To
whom as occasion requires let helpe
be giuen, that they maye serue without murmuring. And when the haue
lesse imployment, let them goe forth
to labour, where they shall be appointed. And not only in these, but in all
other

other offices in the Monaſtery, let this
conſideration be had, that when they
want helpe it be giuen them, and when
they ar vacant , they obeye and doe
what is commanded them. And for the
lodgings of the gueſts , let care there of
be commended to a brother , whoſe
ſoule the feare of God poſſeſſeth ,
where let there be a ſufficient number
of beds made , and let the houſe of
God be wiſely gouerned by diſcreet
men. . And let not any but ſuch
as ar appointed aſſociate himſelfe, or
talke with the gueſts. But if the ſhall
meete or ſee them, humbly ſaluting
them and asking their benediction, let
him paſſe by , ſaying that it is not lawfull for him to talke with a gueſt.

Whether it be lawfull for a Monke to re-
ceaue letters or tokens.

Chap. LIV.

LEt not a monke in noe wiſe ſend
or receaue letters tokens or any
pre-

prefents neyther from his parents, or any other man whatfoeuer or from one an other without the leaue of his Abbot. And if any thinge be fent to him euen from his parente, let him not prefume to receaue it, vnleffe it bee hrft told the Abbot, and if he command that it shall be receaued, let it be in the Abbots power to appoint to whom it shall be giuen, and let not the brother be contriftated to whom it was fent, that their be noe occation giuen to the Deuill. And whofoeuer shall prefume to doe otherwife, let him be lyable to regular difcipline.

Of the cloathes and shooes of the Brethren.

Chap. LV.

LEt cloathes be giuen to the brethren according to the quality of the places where they dwell, or temperature of the aire : Becaufe in cold countryes ther is neede of more, and in

E   hotte

hotte countryes of les. Let it therefore
be in the Abbots power to order this.
Not withstandinge for temperate
places, we thinke it will be sufficiēt for
each Monke to haue a coule and a
cassoke, a coule in the winter haueing
a high nap, in the sommer smoth or old,
and a scapular for worke, shooes and
stockings to put one their fett; and for
the colour or coursenez of these things,
let not the Monks finde fault, but let
them be such as can be prouided in the
prouince in which they dwell, or such
as maye be bought at a cheaper rate.
And let the Abbot see to the measure
and decentnes of these garments, that
they be not to litle for such as vse them,
but of a fitt size. When they receaue
them, let them allwayes restore the old
to be layd vp in the wardrope for the
poore: for it is sufficient for a Monke
to haue two cassockes & two coules
for the nights, for washing and chãge.
Now what is ouer & aboue is super-
fluous, and must be cute of. And as is
said, let them restore what soeuer is old
when

when they receaue new. Let those
who goe à Iourney take breeches out
of the wardrope, and when they returne let them restore them back
washed. And let the coules & cassockes at such times be better then
those they ordinaryly vse , which
goeing a Iorney they take out of
the wardope & returning restore.

For bedding may suffice a straw bed,
a quilt bed, a couerlet , & a pillow,
which beds are often to be searched by
the Abbot , least there be any propriety , and if any be found to haue any
thinge which he hath not receaued
from the Abbot, let him be liable to
most sharp discipline. And that this
vice of propriety maye be rooted out,
let all things be giuen by the Abbot
which shall be necessary, that is a coule,
a cassocke, shoes, stockens a paire of
sleeues, a knife, a steele, a needle , a
handkerchefe, table bookes, that all
excuse of necessity maye be taken a-
waye. Let the Abbot not with standing
alwayes consider the sentence of the

acts

acts of the Apostles, there was giuen
to euery one accordinge as they had
need. And let him therefore consider
the infirmities of such as want, not the
ill will of such as enuie, And in all his
ordinances let him thinke of the retri-
bucion of God.

Of the Abbots table.

CHAP. LVI.

LEt the Abbots table be alwayes
with the guests and strangers. Yet
when there are noe guests, let it be
in his power to call which of the brethren he please. But let him prouide
that there be alwayes one or two of
the seniors left with the brethren by
reason of discipline.

Of

*Of the artificers of the Mo-
nastery.*

Chap. LVII.

IF there be artificers in the Monastery, let them exercise those arts with
all humility and reuerence, if soe be the
Abbot command. But if any of them be
proud of the knowledge he hath in his
art, because he maye seeme to get some
what by it for the Monastery, let him
be taken from it, and let him not exercise it againe; vnlesse after his humilia-
tion the Abbot shall permitt him. And
if any thinge of the worke of the artificers be to be sold, let them by whose
hands they ar to passe take heed, least
they presume to deceaue in any thinge.
Let them remember Ananias & Saphira least the death which they suf-
fered in body, these who committ frau-
din the goode of the Monastery suffer
in their soule. And in the prices and
valuations, let not the vice of auarice
E 3   creepin,

creep in, but let things be allways fold
fome what cheaper then by feculars,
that God may be glorified in all
things.

Of the manner of receauinge
Nouices.

CHAP. LVIII.

IF any one come newly to conuerfion let him not eafyly be admitted.
But as the Apoftle faith, let fpirits be
tryed whether they be from God. If
therefore comming he shall perfeuer
knockinge, and shall be feene for foure
or fiue days patiently to indure iniuries
offred him; & the difficulty which is
made of his entrance, and to perfift in
his petition, then grant him entrance,
and let him be in the cell of the guefts
for a few dayes. And afterwards let
him be in the cell of the nouices, where
he is to meditate, eate, and fleep, and let
fuch a fenior be deputed ouer him, who
is fitt to gaine foules, who muft cu-
riouffy

riouſly & carefully looke to him, to
ſee whether he truly ſeeke God : and
if he be carefull in the ſeruice of God,
in obedience, & in ſuffering reproches.
Let there be ſuggeſted to him the ri-
gor & auſterity by which we tend towards God. And if he promiſe ſtabili-
ty and perſeueráce, after two moneths
ſpace let this rule be read to him in
order, and let there beſaid to him. Behold the lawe vnder which thou deſi-
reſt to fight, if thou canſt obſerue it
enter in, if thou canſt not, freely depart. If he ſhall ſtill perſeuer, then let
him be brought in to the afore ſayd
cell of the nouices, and let him be a-
gaine tryed in all patience. And after
the ſpace of ſix moneths, let the Rule
be read againe to him that he may
know to what he enters in. And if he
ſtill perſeuer, after foure moneths
let the Rule be read againe to him. And
if vppon deliberation had with himſelfe he ſhall promiſe that he will keepe
and obſerue all things commanded
him, then let him be receaued in to the

E 4 Con-

Conuent, knowing himselfe from that
time forward to be vnder the law of
the Rule, foe that it is not lawfull for
him to goe out of the Monaftery, nor
shake of the yoke of the Rule which
he might eyther haue refufed or em-
braced after foe longe deliberation.

And when they admitt him to profeffion let him in the oratorie before,
all, make a promife of his ftability, and
conuerfion of his manners, and obedience before God & his faints, that if
at any time he shall doe otherwife, he
may know that he shall be condemned
by him whom he mocketh. Of which
promife let him make a petition in the
name of thofe faints whofe reliques
are there, & of the Abbot there prefent, which petition let him writte
whith his owne hand, or if he can not
writte, let an other requefted by him
writte it; and the nouice himfelf put to
his figne, and let him lay it on the alter
with his owne hand; which when he
hath done let him prefently beginne
this verfe. *Sufcipe me Domine fecundum*
                                    eloquium

eloquium tuum & viuam, & non confundas me ab expectatione mea. Which verſe let all the conuent anſwer the third tyme, addinge to it *Gloria Patri, &c.* Thē let the ſayd brother nouice proſtrate himſelf at the feet of all, that they maye praye for him : and from that hower let him be accounted one of the conuēt. If he haue anyt hinge, let him either firſt beſtowe it on the poore, or by a ſolemne donation giue it to the Monaſtery, reſeruing for himſelfe nothinge at all, becauſe from that daye forwards he muſt know that he ſhall not haue power as much as ouer his owne body. Let him therefore preſently in the oratorie be ſtript of his owne garments where with he is cloathed, and let him be cloathed with the garments of the Monaſtery. And let thoſe garments which are put of, be layd in the wardrope to be kept. That if at any time by the deuills perſwaſion he conſent to goe out of the Monaſtery, (which God forbid) then taking from him the habit of the Monaſtery, he maye be
turned

turned out, But that writing which the
Abbot tooke of the altar, let him not
haue againe, but let it be kept in the
Monastery.

Of the sonnes of Noblemen or Poore men
which are offred.

CHAP. LIX.

IF perhaps any noble man offers his
sonne to God to liue in the monastery: if the childe himselfe, be vnder
age, let his parents make the fore said
petition or writing for him, and offring
him let them wrap the said petition &
the hand of the childe in the pall of
the altar, & soe let them offer him vp.
And for his goods, let them either in
the said petition promise vnder oath
that they will neuer by themselues
nor by any other person or meās whatsoeuer, either giue him any thinge, or
giue him occasiō of hauing any thinge.
And if they will not doe this, but
will rather offer vp some thing in
allmes

allmes to the monastery, for their greater merit, let them make a donation of
that which they will giue to the monastery, reseruing (if they soe please)
the vse or profit of it for themselues.
But let thinges be soe ordered that noe
suspition remayne with the child, by
which being deceaued he may perish,
(which God forbid) as in others we
haue learned by experience. And in
like manner let the poorer sort doe. But
let them who haue nothing at all simply make their petition, and with an
oblation giue vp theyr sonne before
witnesses.

*Of Priests who desire to dwell in the
Monastery.*

Chap. LX.

IF any that hath taken the order of
Priesthood, shall request to be receued into the monastery, let him not
easily be admitted, yet if he shall still
perseuer in this request, let him know
that

that he is to keepe all difcipline and
obferuance appointed in the Rule, neither shall any thinge be remitted him,
according to that which is written.
Friend for what art thou come: Not
with standing let it be granted him to
ftande next after the Abbot, & to bleffe
& fay maffe if the Abbot doe foe command, otherwife, let him in noe fort
prefume to doe any thinge, knowing
himfelfe fubie&t to regular difcipline,&
let him rather shew to others examples of humility. If perhaps he be in
the Monaftery for fome treaty of ordination, or other occafion whatfoeuer.
Let him remember the place due
to him according to the time of his entrance in to the Monaftery, not that
which is granted him for the reuerence
of Preſthood: And if any other clergy-
man shall likewife defire to be admitted in to the Monaftery, let him be
ranked in a reafonable place, yet foe
that he promife obferuance of the Rule
& ftability in it.

of

Of Monks that be strangers how they ar to be receaued.

CHAP. LXI.

IF any strange Monke shall come from farr places and desire to dwell in the Monastery as a guest, and will be content with the customes of the place which he findeth, & doth not trouble the Monastery with his super-fluityes, but is well contented with what he findeth, let him be entertay-ned for as long time as he desireth. And if he reasonably and with humility and charity reprehend or admonish any thing, let the Abbot prudently consider what he sayth, for perhaps our Lord sent him for that end. And if after he desire to make his abode there, let him not be refused, especially, because in the time while he liued à guest, his life might be sufficiently knowne. But if in that time he be found giuen to su-perfluity or vitiousnes, let him not only

be

be refufed, but alfo let him be ciuilly
bid to depart, leaft others be corrupted
by hisili demeanure. But if he be not
fuch à one as deferueth to be caft out,
let him not only if he demande it, be
receaued into the fociety of the conuent, but let him be perfuaded to ftay,
that by his exemple others may be in-
ftructed, becaufe in euery place we
ferue one God and fight vnder one
kinge; And if the Abbot shall find him
to be well deferuing, he may alfo place
him in a higher rank. And not only a
Monke he may thus exalt aboue his
time in the habit, but alfo any of the
aforefaid degrees of Priefts or Clergie
men, if their lifes deferue it. But let the
Abbot beware, leaft at any time he receaue a Monke of an other knowne
Monaftery to dwell, without the confent of his Abbot or letters of com-
mendation from him : becaufe it is
written what thou wilt not haue dóne
to thy felfe, doe not to an other.

Of

Of the Priests of the Monastery.

CHAP. LXII.

IF any Abbot desire to haue a Priest or Deacon ordered, let him choose one that is worthy of the function of Priesthood. And let him who is ordered beware of haughtines and pride, neither let him presume to doe any thinge but what is commanded him by the Abbot, knowing him selfe to be much more subiect to regular discipline. Not by reason of his Priesthood let him forget the obedience & discipline of the Rule, but let him striue more & more to goe forwards towards God. And let him always consider the place which is due to him according to the time of his entrance in to the Monastery, although perhaps by the election of the conuent & the will of the Abbot, he be promoted for the good desert of his life. And let him know

that

obſerue
Deans
preſume
iudged
rebel-
beinge
p alſo
r all
at his
us, let
lery; in
s that he
bey the

g4

orders in
ne of cõ-
res, or as
let not
commit-
ge free
power,

holy
power, ord
let him al
giue accou
ments, and
ding to the
Which the
felues , Le
the commu
ftand in th
whatfoeu
the order,
Becaufe S
dren, iudg
ting, tho
the Abbo
prefer or
ferue the
(for exar
the fecōd
himfelfe
nior , wh
the day,
he be.

And l
of difciplin
Iuniors h

niors loue their Iuniors. And in the
callinge of their name, let it not be
lawfull for any one to call an other by
his plaine name, but let the feniors call
the Iuniors brothers, and the Iuniors
call their feniors *Domni*, which fignifieth à fatherly reuerence. And let the
Abbot becaufe he reprefenteth the per-
fon of Chrift be called *Domnus*, and
Abbot not as affuming it himfelfe, but
giuen him for the honour & loue of
Chrift. And let him remember to
carry him felfe fo, as he may be worthy
of fuch honour. And where fouer the
brethren meet one an other, let the iunior aske benediction of the antient,
and the antient paffing by, let the iunior rife and giue him place to fitt: neither let the iunior prefume to fit with
him, vnleffe his fenior command him,
to full fill that which is written, pre-
uenting each other with honour. Let
the children or younger fort in the oratorie and at the table keep their orders
with difcipline, and abroad or where-
foeuer els let there be carefull watch
ouer

ouer them, that they alwayes keep good order vntill they come to age of vnderstanding.

Of ordaining the Abbot.

CHAP. LXIV.

IN the ordaining of the Abbot let allwayes that consideration be had, that he be chosen whom all the conuent with one assent in the feare of God, or elsa part of the cōuent though otherwise small with mature aduice shall choose. And let him who is to be ordered or consecrated be chosen for his good desert of life, learning, and wisdome, though he be the last in the conuent. And if the whole conuent (which God forbid) shall with one consent choose à person consenting to their vices: and the vices themselues shall by some means or other come to bee made knowne to the Bishop, (to whose diocese that place appertay-neth) or to the Abbots or christians

r

ier the con-
om preuay-
ny fteward
owing that
e a good re-
pure inten-
od as on the
if they ne.

iained, muft
ien he hath
ne is to giue
p ; and let
behouefull
ers , then to
t behoueth
rned in the
know from
w thinges &
ercifull, and
prefer mer-
he himfelfe
le mufthate
, and in cor-
gorous or ex-
kes to fcoure
the

the veſſeil he breake it. And let him allwayes ſuſpect his owne frailty, & remember that a shaken reed is not to be broken. By this we would ſaye, not that he ſuffer vice to be noriſhed, but that with prudence and charity he ſeek to roote them out, in ſuch manner as he ſees to be moſt expedient, & let him ſtudy to bee more loued then feared. Let him not be turbulent or ſad, neyther let him be ſuperfluous & obſtinat nor jelous, or ouer ſuſpicious: forthen he will neuer be at quiet. In his commands let him be prudent and conſiderat; whether they be thinges pertaining to God or to the world. Let him conſider well, and moderat the worker which he inioyneth, haueing in minde the diſcretiō of holy Iacob who ſayed. If I shall make my flockes to labour ouer much in goeinge, They will all dye in one daye. Hauing therefore theſe and other teſtimonies of diſcretion, the mother of vertues, let him ſo temper all thinges, that both the ſtrong maye deſire to accomplish, and the weake maye mayenot shrinke backe from vndertaking what is commanded. And especially that he obserue this present Rule in all thinges: that when he shall haue serued well, he may heare from our Lord what the good seruant heard, who gaue corne to his fellow seruants in his tyme. Amen. I say vnto you, ouer all his goods he will place him.

*Of the Prepositus of the Mo
nastery.*

Chap. LXV.

IT often tymes happens that by the ordaining of the prepositus great scandalls arise in Monasteries; whiles there are some puffed vp with the malignant spirit of pride, who esteeming themselues to be second Abbots, & taking vppon them to tyránice ouer others, nourish scandalls and make dissentions in the conuent, and especially in those places, where by the same Bishop or Abbots, which ordaine
the

the Abbot, the prepositus is likewise ordained, which how vnfitting a thinge it is, may easily be perceaued : Becaufe from the very begining of his ordina-tion there is occation giuen him of being proud : his thoughtes suggesting to him that he is exempt from the Ab-bot, Becaufe he is ordained by them by whom the Abbot himfelfe is ordained. Hence arife enuies, chidings, detrac-tions, emulations, diffentions & difor-ders:& whileft the Abbot and the Pro-pofitus are at variance, it muft needs be that both their foules runn a hazard in this diffention : & thofe who are vn-der their charge, whiles they adhere to parties and runn into perdition. The fault of which danger lyeth principal-ly vpon them who were the authors of fuch an ordination.

And therefore wee fore fee that it is expedient for the conferuation of peace and charity, that the whole gouernment of the Monaftery depend of the Abbots will : and if it can be donne, let it be gouerned by Denes; as
before

before we haue ordained, that whiles
the charge is committed to many one
be not made proud. But if either the
place requier it, or the conuent shall
reasonably & with humility demand
it. And the Abbot iudge it expedient,
whomsoeuer the Abbot shall choose
by the counselle of his brethrē fearing
God, let him ordaine for his Prepositus. And let the Prepositus doe those
thinges with reuerence, which shall be
inioyned him by his Abbot : doing nothing against the will or ordinance of
his Abbot, because by how much he
is preferred before the rest, by soe
much it be houeth him carefully to
obserue the precepts of the Rule.
Which Prepositus if he shall be found
vitious, or seduced by the haughtines
of pride, or be founde a contemner of
the holy rule, let him be admonished
with words till foure times, & if he doe
not amend, let the correction of regular discipline be giuen him. And if
with that he amende not, let him be
deposed from the dignity of Prepositus-
ship,

ship, & let an other who is worthy, be substituted in his place. And if afterwards he be not quiet & obedient in the conuent, let him then be expelled the Monastery. Yet let the Abbot consider that he is to giue an account to God of all his actions, least perhaps his soule be inflamed with enuy or emulation.

Of the Porter of the Monastery.

Chap. LXVI.

AT the gate of the Monastery let there be placed a wise old man, who knowes how to receaue and giue an answere: whose age may not suffer him to wander, which Porter ought to haue his cell neer the gate: that commers may alwayes find one ready to returne them an answer. And by and by assone as any one shall knocke, or à poore man shal crye, let him answer Deo gratias; and with all mildenes

F

nes & feare of God let him prefently
giue an anfwere with all charity. And
let the porter if he need for his comfort, haue a Iunior brother with him.
The Monaftery if it can conueniently,
ough fo to be built, that all neceffa-
ries, to witt watter, a mill, a garden, a
Bakehoufe, and other feuerall artes
maye be had and practiced in the Monaftery, that their be noe neceffity for
the monkes to wander abroad, becaufe
it is in noe fort expedient for their
foules. And we will haue this Rule
often read in the conuent, leaft any of
the Brethren excufe himfelfe of ignorance.

Of Brethren that be fent a
Iourney.

CHAP. LXVII.

LEt the Brethren that are to be fent
à Iourney, commend themfelues
to the prayers of all theyr brethren, &
of the Abbot, & alwayes at the laft
prayer

prayer of the worke of God, let commemoration of all the abfent be made. And let the Brethren retourninge from a Iourney in the very day in which they returne, at all the canonicall houres when the worke of God is ended, proftrate on the grounde in the oratorie, and defier the prayers of all for their excefses, leaft perchance either any fight or hearing of fome euill thing, or any idle fpeech haue ftole vpon them in the way. And let not any prefume to tell others what thinges he hath feene or hard abroad with out the Monaftery, Becaufe it is a great diftraction to them. And if any shall prefume to doe it, let him be liable to regular punishment. And likwife he that shall prefume to goe without the cloyfters of the Monaftery, or to goe any whither, or doe any thinge though neuer foe litle without the command of the Abbot.

If

If impoſsible thinges be enioyned to à
Brother.

CHAP. LXVIII.

IF any hard or impoſſible thinges be
inioyned any Brother, let him receaue the command of the bidder with
all mildnes & obediēce. And if he shall
ſee that the burden altogether exceeds
the meaſure of his ſtrength, let him patiently & fitly ſuggeſt the cauſes of the
impoſſibility thereof to him is ouer
him, not shewing any pride or contra-
diction, & if after his ſuggeſtion, the
Prior or antient shall perſiſt in commanding it, let the Iunior know, that it
is expedient for him : & let him out of
charity obey, truſtinge in the aſſiſtance
of God.

That

That one preſume not to defend an other
in the Monaſtery.

CHAP. LXIX.

THere muſt ſpeciall heed be taken
that vpon no occaſion, one monke
preſume to defend or maintaine another in the Monaſtery, though they be
neuer ſoe neare of kine, let none of
them I ſay preſume to doe this in any
ſorte : becauſe from thence exceeding
great occaſion of ſcandalle may ariſe.
And if any ſhall tranſgreſſe in this
point let him be ſeuerely puniſhed.

That noe one preſume to beat or excom-
municate an other.

CHAP. LXX.

THat occaſion of all preſumption
may be auoyded in the Monaſ-
tery, we ordaine and conſtitute, that it
be not lawfull for any one to excom-

muni-

municate or beat any of his brethren, except those who haue power and autority from the Abbot. And let those that offende bee reprehended before all, that the rest may be afraide. But ouer Infants vntil they be fifteen yeers of age, let their bee strict discipline & care had by all ; yet this also with discretion & measure. For he who shall in any sort presume to doe any thinge to such as are of riper years without the command of the Abbot, or shall be vndiscreetly seuere euen to Infants, let him be liable to regular discipline, because it is written. What thou wilt not haue donne to thy selfe, doe not doe to an other.

That the Brethren be obedient to each other.

CHAP. LXXI.

OBediēce is not only to be yeelded to the Abbot, but also the brethrē ar to obey one an other, knowing
that

that by this kinde of obedience they
shallgoe to God. The command therefore of the Abbot or other superiours
conſtituted by him being firſt obey'd,
before which we ſuffer not priuat commandes to be prefered, in other thinges
let the Iuniors obey their elders with
all charity and diligence. And if any
be found contentious, let him be rebuked. And if a Brother be rebuked,
for any euen the leaſt thinge by the
Abbot, or by any of his ſeniors, or if
he ſhall but perceaue the mind of his
ſenior, to be troobled or moued againſt
him, though but a litle, let him without delaye proſtrate at his feete, and
there lye till that commotion be ap-
peaſed with Bleſſing, and if any one
ſhall contemne to doe it, let him be
eyther liable to corporall puniſhment,
or if he be contumatious, let him be
expelled the Monaſtery.

Of

Of the good zeale which Monkes ought to haue.

CHAP. LXXII.

AS there is an il zeale of bitternes which seperateth from God, & leadeth to hell : soe there is a good zeale which seperateth from vices, & leadeth to God and life euerlasting. Let Monkes therefore exercise this zeale with most feruent loue, that *is*, that they preuent each other with honour, that they paciently suffer each others infirmityes, whether they be of body or of minde, and that they striue to obey each other. Let none follow that which he thinks profitable for himselfe; but rather what others thinke fitting. Let them shew all brotherly charity with a chast loue. Let them feare God, and loue their Abbot with a sincere and humble affection, and prefer nothing at all before Christ, who

vouchsafe

vouchſafe to bringe vs all to life e-
uerlaſting Amen.

That all obſeruance of Iuſtice is not ſett
downe in this Rule.

Chap. LXXIII.

VVEe haue writt this Rule
that by obſeruinge it in
Monaſteries, wee may ſhew ourſelues
to haue in ſome meaſure either ho-
neſtie of manners, or the beginning of
a good conuerſation. But for thoſe
who haſten to the perfection of holy
conuerſation, there ar the preceps of
the holy farhers: he obſeruance whereof bringeth à man to the height of perfection. For what ſide of a leafe, or
what word of diuine authority of the
old and new teſtament, is not a moſt
ſtraight ruie of mans life, or what
booke of the holy Catholike fathers
doth not ſound forth this, that we may
come by a direct courſe to our Crea-
tor. Moreouer the Collations of the
fathers

fathers & their inftitutes & liues, alfo the Rule of our holy father Bafil, what els are they but examples of well liuing, & obediente monkes and inftruments of vertues. But to vs flouthfull ill liuing and negligent people, they are a shame and confufion. whofoeuer therefore thou art, who haftens to the heauenly country, obferue by the helpe of Chrift this litle Rule writt for beginners : and then atlength by the protection of God thou shalt come to thofe higher perfections of doctrine, & vertues of which we haue before fpoken. To fuch as fullfill thefe things the kingdone of heauen shalle lye open. Amen.

F I N I S.

A SHORT TREATISE

TOVCHING THE CONFRATERNITIE

OF THE SCAPVLAR OF

St. BENEDICTS ORDER.

Fraternitatem diligite. Loue the Fraternitie or Brother-hood. 1. Pet. 2. 17.

Permiſſu Superiorum.
Anno Do. 1639.

TO THE RIGHT HONORABLE

THOMAS

LORD WINDESOR.

MY LORD.

This declineinge age of the world, is soe posest and transported with à malignant critique humor, abstractinge from greater vices, and errors; that venerable truth, (how euer cloathed

* 2   *with*

with the candid garments of in-
nocency , warranted with the
testimonies, and practize of in-
numerable Saincts , togeather
with the vniuersall currend of
Catholique Doctors in all ages)
can not appeare in publique, especially in our miserable cuntrie,
without imminent daunger of
beinge decrid and supprest , by
such as little care to be wicked,
soe they may be reputed witty:
This hath imposed vpon me
(beinge for obedience to publish
this little treatise) the happy necessity of haueinge recourse to
your Lordship that it may
find à refuge vnder the protection

tion of your most honorable
name, to sheild it from the blas-
tinge ayre of such infected Spirits. The worke (I must confes
our many obligations considered) is in appearance too small
and worthles, for à person of soe
emminent and noble quality:
But since there are peculiar
reasons knowne to vs, which
exact that in all iustice and prudence, especially at this tyme,
this booke of our confraternity,
ought rather to be dedicated to
your Lordship then any other:
and since with all the cause and
matter are of their owne nature
sacred, the hazards which it is

        * 3   to

to paſſe many, and that all worthy men are interreſted, wheare
truth is expoſed to the venture
of ſuffrance, (à patrone therefore beinge abſolutely neceſſa-
ry, who is both good greate and
learned) ſince moreouer the happines of princes conſiſts not a-
lone in the lardge extent of their
dominions, but much rather in
the affection and fidelitie of
their frends & ſubiects: And fi-
naly ſince this little cõfraternitie
comes not alone, but brings with
it, many harts vnited in charity,
all which with à loueinge but
moſt humble ſincerity, are a vo-
luntarie ſacrifice to the ſchrine

of

DEDICATORIE

of your admirable vertues, inclu-
dinge not alone the mutuall ſer-
uices of all our poor company,
as it is now exiſtant, but with
all the merrits and prayers of
many thouſands, who once wore
the ſame liuery vpon earth, and
are now glorious fauourites in
the court of heauen: it is manifeſt, that on the one ſide it weare
no meane impiety, and much
greater inciuilitie, to conſecrate
it to any other hand, then his,
who hath by ſoe many, and ſoe
iuſt titles made it his owne, togeather with our ſelues: on the
other we haue infinite incoura-
gements to perſwade, that your
                              exellent

excellēt difpofition & wifdome,
will efteeme of it accordinge to
the reall worth, which is not
confind alone to the letter, but
rather extends it felfe to many
fpiritual preheminences, which
farre tranfcend the capacity of
thofe who want your Lordships
faith and fcience : or if this
want waight, atleaft the pious
intentions of a familie, once the
moft powerfull vpon earth, ten-
dinge to doe your Lordship all
honnor deferues acceptance, fince
we obleige our felues by this act
to remaine for euer your beads
men. Accept therefore my honorable good lord this fmall pledge
of

DEDICATORIE

of many greate desires, and be-
pleased with all to excuse the mã-
ner of expreßion, which sauours
rather of scholes then the courte,
it is well knowne from whence
it came, and therefore I am con-
fident will be gratefully receiued without further appologie.
This fauour will add to our many obligations, and amongst the
rest binde me the most vnworthy
to remaine.

Your honors
most humble seruant,
A. B.

APPROBATIO.

THis threefold treatife contayning the life and Rule of our Holy Father St. Bennet, and the Confraternity of his holy Order, hath beene read and approued by learned men of our Congregation; and therefore we giue licence that it be printed. Giuen at Doway this 27. th of Auguft. 1639.

  B. CLEMENT Reyner Prefident Generall of the English Benedictine Congregation.

A SHORT TREATISE

TOVCHING THE CONFRATERNITIE

OF THE SCAPVLAR OF

St. BENEDICTS ORDER.

Fraternitatem diligite. Loue the Frater-nitie or Brotherhood. 1. PET. 2. 17.

THE PREFACE TO THE READER.

GENTLE READER,

Some of the most ancients of the Fathers of our holy Order and Con-gregatiõ hauing vnderstood, that these two small treatises, to witt the Rule of St. Bennet, and the Dialogues of St.

A   GRE

Gregory, expressing his life, were to be
printed, desired me (to whom the care
of hauing them printed was cōmitted)
to adioine vnto them the letters of Fraternitie, by which some few of our
speciall friends & benefactors are made
partakers of all our suffrages, sacrifices,
masses, praiers, fastings, disciplines, and
of all other our laborious actions, and
passions, and good workes whatsoeuer
we doe; with the forme obserued by superiours when they grant these graces
to anie one; and with à verie briefe, yet
cleare declaration of the principall difficulties which are obiected by those
who vnderstand not the sayd letters
rightly. All which I presently signi-
fied to our right R^d. Fa. President,
(without whose leaue nothing may be
printed by anie of ours) requesting that
he would cōmende the matter to some
bodie of greater sufficiency then I take
my selfe to be. But he conceauing far
better of me (it seemes) then I desire (as
I feare will appeare too clearly in this
ensuing little treatise) commāded me to
sett vppon the worke without delay,
                                                and

and to dispatch it out of hand which I
herenow do, hoping that if anie thing
be à misse, or short of the sufficiency
which he expects, eyther he will amend
it, or thou (gentle Reader) pardon it,
seeing I haue done the best I could to
content all.

A SHORT TREATISE

TOVCHING THE CONFRATERNITIE

OF THE SCAPVLAR OF

St. BENEDICTS ORDER.

CHAPTER I.

Containing the letters of Con-
fraternitie.

 EFORE I begin to treat of
other matters promised in
my preface, it will be necef-
farie to set downe the tenour
of the letters of our Confraternitie
which is as followeth.

Br. N. N.

Br. N. N. of the holy Order of St.
bennet, and generall Prefident of the
Congregation of England of the fame
Order, to the (N. N.) grace and happines in our Lord and Sauiour Iefus
Chrift. The bleffed Apoftle St. Paule
telleth vs, that there are noe Sacrifices
more powerfull to deferue the loue and
protection of our mercifull Redeemer,
then the workes of mercie & communication one to another, the fpirituall
and temporall graces which God almightie imparteth vnto vs. For which
caufe our holy Order hath accuftomed
to admit vnto the participation of all
graces and meritts, that by the helpe of
God abound in it, fuch worthy perfons,
as by conftant profeffion of the Catholique faith, and true endeauour of vertuous life, and carefull exercife of the
workes of charitie, edifie the companie
of Gods Church, and helpe forward
their weaker or poorer neighbours in
the way of faluation. For which re-
fpects, efpeciallie that you haue defired
it at our hands, we haue thought good
to giue vnto you this letter of Frater-
                                nitie

nitie for your selfe : by which letters,
through the power graunted vnto vs
by the Apostolicall Sea , and from our
generall Chapter, we do make you partaker of all the graces and meritts of
our Order , admitting and accepting of
you into the number of our Brethren
and benefactors , and communicating
vnto you freelie and willinglie from
our hearts, the participation and en-
ioying of all suffrages , sacrifices, and
Masses, prayers and fastings, disciplines
and almesdeedes, studies , sermons, recollections and meditations, mortifications and obediences , and all other labours, actions and passions , and good
workes whatsocuer haue or shall be
exercised by helpe of Gods grace in v-
nion of our Sauiour Christ his meritts
and satisfactions , for the honour and
glorie of God almightie , now and in
your life time , and after it shall please
God to call you out of this world vnto
his mercie. Confiding that by the
goodnes of God allmightie, and the in-
tercession of his holy mother, & all his
glorious Angells and Saints , particu-

A 3   larly

larly of our holy Patriarch St. Bennet,
and his Sister St. Scholastic & his admirable childrē St. Gregorie the great,
St. Augustine our Apostle, St. Maurus,
St. Placidus, St. Romuald, St. Bernard,
St. Celestine, and diuers founders of
sundrie Congregations vnder St. Bennets Rule. St. Florentine St. Gertrude,
St. Hildegardis, St. Etheldreda, St.
Eadburg, St. Francisca of Rome, & infinite other Sainčts of both sexe, which
for the space of twelue hundred yeares
florished in our Order, enriched the
Church with learning and example, &
peopled heauē with their persons. This
our graunt and letter of Fraternitie or
Brotherhood will be profitable to your
soule, and à helpe to encrease in you all
good duties and vertuous endeauours.
Giuing you particularlie to vnderstand,
that to enioy these things, you are to
weare in secret à little scapular blessed
by vs, and euerie night examining your
conscience, and by that examination
procuring to place your selfe in that
disposition of mind and affection, in
which by Gods grace you would not

f₂ae

feare to die; and after saying thrice ouer
à Pater, and Aue, and once à Creed, for
the exaltation and happie successe of
the Catholicque, Apostolicque, and
Romane Church, you shall for euerie
time thus doing obtaine remission for
à yeare and quarentall of penance, o-
therwise due, or enioyned for your
sinnes, and hauing confessed with har-
tie contrition and sorrow, and allso
cõmunicated and receiued the Sacrament of the Altar once à month, you
shall euerie time so doing once à môth,
obtaine à plenarie indulgence and en-
tire forgiuenesse of all penances & pu-
nishments due for your offences. And
if at the hower of your death you vo-
callie repeat from your heart the sweet
name of Iesus, or not being able to pronounce it with your mouth, reuolue it
deuoutlie & reuerentlie in your mind,
you shall obtaine full remission of your
sinnes; and the selfe same Indulgences
you shall obtaine, causing for your deuotion and charitie three Masses to be
offered for the deliuerance of the soule
of any departed brother thus admitted
                                    into

into our fraternitie; not doubting allso
but you of your part will assist vs with
your praiers, merits, and good workes,
and will procure to performe such holy exercises as you shall see practised
by such as are of your brotherhood, so
farre forth as you may without hinderance or incōmoditie of your other
obligations of your calling, and exercise of your priuate deuotions. In wit-
nes of all which we haue in the name
of the Father, sonne, and holy Ghost
one true immortall, and most mercifull
God in three cōsubstantiall persons,
giuen this our letter of Confraternitie,
and sealed it with our seale, vnder our
owne hand, & the subscription of our
Secretarie.

CHAPTER II.

*Expressing the manner of admittance in to
the Confraternitie.*

1. NExt is to describe and sett
downe to the view of the
world the manner, forme, and Cere-
monies,

monies, how brethren and sisters are
wont to be admitted into our Confraternitie. And for this purpose, I will
now cite word for word the 28.29.30.
and 31. numbers of the eight Chapter
of our Constitutions for the Mission of
England, where this sayd forme is described in latine; which it will be need-
lesse to English, being it concerneth
only or chieflie, the function of the
priest, who is to blesse and giue the Scapular.

2, Non admittantur facile ad beneficium confraternitatis, nisi qui virtutum
meritis eo digni inuenientur, quique
dicto beneficio ad laudem Dei ordinis-
que decus præsumuntur vsuri: nec qui-
uis promiscue hoc beneficium conferat
etiam dignis, sed Præses tantu, aut Pro-
uinciales & Priores, aut alij duntaxat
pauci ab ipsis ad hoc deputati.

3. Confrater aut consoror antequam
scapulari vestiatur debebunt accuratè
confessionis sacramentum saltem præ-
mittere, & si commode poterunt etiam
sacram communionem : deinde com-
modo tempore astantibus paucis fideli-
bus

bus ac deuotis amicis, ipso genu flexo
qui beneficium habitus est sumpturus
benedicat sacerdos scapulare vt sequi-
tur.

Verf. Adiutorium nostrum in nomine
    Domini.

Resp. Qui fecit cælum & terram.

Verf. Domine exaudi orationem meam.

Resp. Et clamor meus ad te veniat.

Verf. Dominus vobiscum.

Resp. Et cum spiritu tuo.

OREMVS.

ÆTerne pater, Omnipotens Deus
qui vnigenitum tuum, Dominũ
nostrum Iesum Christum nostræ mor-
talitatis fragilem vestem induere volui-
sti: obsecramus immensam largitatis
tuæ abundantiam, vt benedictionem
tuam in hunc sacrum habitum effun-
dere digneris: vt sicut ipsum Sancti Pa-
tres nostri ad innocentiæ & humilitatis
indicium à renunciantibus sæculo san-
xerunt gestendum; ita benedictione tua
fiat, vt quicunque eo deuotè & fideliter
                                    vsus

vſus fuerit ob nominis tui gloriam &
Sancti ſerui tui Benedicti Patris noſtri
deuotionem ipſum Dominū noſtrum
Ieſum Chriſtum induere mereatur. Per
cundem Dominum noſtrum Ieſum
Chriſtum. Amen.

4 Deinde aſpergat aquâ benedictâ
& conuerſus ad eum qui induendus eſt
moneat ipſum hâc ſuſceptionê aſtringi
ad ordinem. S. Benedicti peculiariter
honorandum & defendendum: & ſpe-
cialiter obligari non tamen ſub pæna
peccati) ad exercitium illud quotidianū
quod in litteris confraternitatis propo-
nitur. Ipſo vero ſynceriter conatum
ſuum pollicente, & adhuc genu flexo
manente, ſacerdos ſcapulare benedictū
accipiat, eique induat dicens.

Accipe iugum Chriſti ſuaue, & onus
eius leue. In nomine Patris, & Filij, &
Spiritus ſancti. Amen.

Deinde aſpergat eum aquâ benedictâ, & ſubiungat.

Authoritate Reuerendi admodum
Patris Præſidis ipſi à ſanctâ Sedê Apo-
ſtolicâ conceſſâ, & in hâc parte mihi
commiſſâ recipio te ad côfraternitatem
no-

nostræ sacræ religionis, & inuesti oac
participem te facio omnium bonorum
spiritualium eiusdem ordinis nostri. In
nomine Dei Patris, & Filij, & Spiritus
Sancti. Amen.

Et adijciat.

Confirma hoc Deus quod operatus
es in nobis à templo sancto tuo quod est
in Ierusalem.

Vers. Dominus vobiscum.

Resp. Et cum spiritu tuo.

OREMVS.

A Desto dulcissime Domine Deus
supplicationibus nostris, & hunc
famulum tuum, quem sacræ nostræ re-
ligioni sociamus, perpetuâ tribue fir-
mitate roborari, vt perseueranti propo-
sito in omni valeat sanctitate tibi fa-
mulari. Per Christum Dominum nostrum. Amen.

5   His expletis litteras confraternitatis ei tradat, nomenque eius in libro
confraternitatis describat.

CHAPTER III.

*Concerning the antiquitie of the foresaid
letters of Fraternitie.*

1   Lthough the general practife
of Religious difperfed ouer
the world were fufficient to shew that
the giuing of fuch letters of Fraternitie
as haue bin fpoake of aboue is no new
inuented noueltie, feing that decourfe
of time & manie reiterated actions are
neceffarily required for the introdu-
cing of an vniuerfal cuftome in all
places; yet I thinke it not amiffe to
fpeake brieflie of the antiquitie of the
faid letters, for as much as concerneth
the Order of St. Bennet in particular.
2. The Monkes therefore of the holy
Order of St. Bennet of the English
Congregation, receaued this cuftome
firft of all from their forefathers the
Apoftles of England as shall be shewed
by and by, and now lately fince their
banishment receaued the fame cuf-
       B   tome

tome againe in imitation of the Spanish
Congregatiō of the same Order, where
out of the 97. writing of their booke of
priuileiges, they found it had bin practised for a long time. This Congregation
had learned the same from the Italian
Monkes of the same Order, by whome
they had beene informed of such
things, as concerned the obseruance of
St. Bennets Rule, and of the customes
of the same Order, of which this was
one as may be seene in their sixt con-
stitution vppon the last chapter of the
same St. Bennets Rule.

3.   The Italian Monkes had learned
this from St. Benet himselfe, and therefore where soeuer they came did intro-
duce it : as for exāple in England where
they first planted the holy Ghospell of
Christ, and the Order of St. Bennet a-
mongst English men, as is related in
the booke called *Apostolatus Benedicti-*
norum in Anglia set forth at the apoint-
ment of the general Chapter by the
R. F. Clement Reyner then Secretarie,
now President Generall of our Congregation, where in the verie end of
the

the Appendix there is mention of admitting Lewes King of France to the
Fraternity of the Monkes of Canter-
bury: and of diuers other remarkable
things to this purpose. The like was
also obserued by the first planters of
our Order in France, where St. Maurus (disciple to our holy Father St. Bennet) gaue such letters of Fraternity to
the King Theodoretus, as Antonius
Yeapes asseuereth in the Chronicles ad
annum 64. Sti. Benedicti. And no wonder, for he had seene St. Bennet himselfe
do the like in receiuing Tertullus St.
Placide his father to the Fraternitie of
his Order, as Surius reciteth in the life
of St. Placide.

4. And if you desire to knowe vpon
what ground St. Bennet did attempt
this, reade if it please you the holy Fathers & scriptures in such places as are
to be cited in this treatise following, &
it will appeare that he had warrant e-
nough for his so doing. And if no other
authoritie could be found; the holy
exāple of Ionathas which is set downe

in the

in the firſt booke of the Machabes 12.
chapter and 6. verſe, had beene ſufficient to warrant him: for there we find
recorded at lardge ſome letters of Fraternitie. (ſo the holy Scripture calls
them) which Ionathas the high prieſt,
Elders, Prieſts, & people of the Iewiſh
nation ſent vnto their brethren of Spar-
tiata.   In which letters they vſe theſe
words : *We therefore at all times with-*
out intermiſsion on ſolemne dayes, and o-
thers, as it behoueth, are mindfull of you
in our Sacrifices, which we offer, and in
our obſeruances, as is religious and fitting
to be mindfull of brethren. What more
can be deſired for the iuſtification of
St. Bennets cuſtome of giuing letters of
Fraternitie ? Other grounds ſhall be
touched here after as occaſion will be
offered in ſoluing of the difficulties
which are commonly obiected againſt
the afore ſayd letters.

CHAP-

Chapter IV.

The first difficultie is concerning the bestowing of Indulgences.

1. NOw I come to the principal point which is to propose and answere such difficulties as either malice or ignorance hath in seuerall ages obiected against this pious custome, not only of our holy Order and Congregation in admitting lay persons vnto our Fraternitie, but of all Orders in generall. In which matter neuertheles my intention is not to stirre vp more difficulties then of necessitie must be handled, for the better vnderstanding of the letters of Fraternitie, which haue beene recited and so often spoakē of before, nor to discusse these difficulties which are to be proposed in such manner as they are hādled in schooles by the learneder sort of schoolemen, because this would be too tedious; but I only intend to moue à doubt and the

B 3   occasion

occasion of it, to propose brieflie the reason of the doubt which is to be discussed, & to touch vppon the solution, with citation of such authors who treate more amply of the same subiect by whose helpe and industrie, an indifferent scholler with verie little labour may (if need be) inlardge this discourse, at his better leasure hearafter.

2.   The first difficultie which I meane to propose shall be, concerning the Indulgences mentioned in the aforesaid letters of Fraternitie, *Wheather that Superiors of Religious Orders haue power to giue Indulgences vnto their friends and benefactors or no?* The occasion of mouing this doubt is taken out of the letters themselues, which to some may seeme to suppose that Superiors haue that power, because they bestow Indulgences verie liberally vpon their friends & benefactors, as may be seene towards the end of the sayd letters, and yet the common opinion of diuines saith the contrarie. For alkhough

some

some do asseuer that not only the Pope, but also euerie particular bisshop hath by the diuine law sufficient power to bestow Indulgences vpon their subiects; yet few or no diuines do mantaine that Superiors of Religious Orders haue the like authoritie. Roderiquez Tom.2. qq. Reg.q.85.a.1. indeed laboureth all he can to shew that such Religious Superiors as haue authoritie like vnto Episcopall authoritie, to wit Prouincialls, Presidents, or Generalls haue the same power to giue Indulgences as Bishops haue. And Medina de Indulgētijs dist.6.cap.29. holds the same. But this maketh nothing to iustifye the practise aboue mentioned, by which we see that Religious Superiors bestow Indulgences on lay people who are not subiect vnto them.

3. This obiection is so weake, that it needs no other confutation then the diligent inspection of the aboue mētioned forme of letters, in which the true solution is so sufficiently declared, that we stand in no need of Roderiquez, or Medina,

Medina , or any of their affociats for
this matter ; becaufe the doctrine deliuered in the letters them felues is cõ-
formable to à knowne truth maintai-
ned by all Catholique diuines, which
is, that the Pope, as head of the Church,
and as vicair of our bleffed Sauiour
Chrift here vpon earth, hath full power
by the diuine law, not only to giue Indulgences vnto the faithfull, but to de-
legate this his power vnto others as he
shall thinke expedient to do : which
truth being fuppofed and graunted,
then you are to note thefe words contained in the à boue mentioned letters:
We haue thought good to giue vnto you
this letters of Confraternitie for your felfe,
by which letters through the power graun-
ted to vs by the Apoftolique Sea &c. By
which the propofed difficultie is fully
folued; for by them the reader may vn-
derftand, that for as much as concerneth Indulgences giuen vnto lay people not fubiect vnto the Superiors of
the Order, the Sea Apoftolique hath
authorifed the Superiors fo to doe by
                                    graun-

graunting them priuiledges to that effect, as may be seene in the 97. priuiledge of the foresayd booke of priuileges graunted to the Spanish Congregation of the holy Order of St. Bennet,
and from them extended vnto our Cōgregation of England.

4. Out of which discourse it maie be
gathered that the Superiors of our
Congregation, may if please thē graunt
farre greater Indulgences to their
friends and benefactors then hitherto
they haue expressed in thier letters of
Fraternitie; seeing that by the priuiledges of Paulus V. and Vrbanus VIII.
they do communicate in priuiledges
with all other Orders and Congregations whatsoeuer, to whome wonderfull great concessions haue beene made
by the Sea Apostolique concerning the
giuing of Indulgēces vnto their friēds,
and benefactors as Hieronymus à Sorbo sheweth in his booke called Compendium priuilegiorum mendicātium,
& non mendicantium; verbo: Indulgentiæ quoad sæculares. 1.

CHAP-

CHAPTER V.

*The second difficultie, is about the appli-
cation of merits.*

1. SOme there were, who thought
themselues no meane men or ordinarie schollers, who haue wonderfully exclamed against Religious Superiors for applying the merits of
their Religious subiects vnto their benefactors, and for applying their benefactors meritts vnto themselues, asseue-
ring that this phrase of speaking is he-
reticall (so bitter they were in their
writings against these & such like letters of Confraternitie.) For which
cause I thought good to propose this
difficultie : *Whether Religious Superiors
can apply to their friends and benefactors,
the merits of their subiects?* and in like
sort : *Whether their friends can apply their
merits and good workes vnto the Religious of that Order or Cōgregation to which
they are vnited.*

                                2.   It

2. It might seeme by the aboue cited letters that they may; for soone after the beginning of them it is sayd:
For which cause our holy Order hath accu-
stomed to admit vnto the participation of
all graces and merits &c. And not farre
frō the end of the sayd letters it is sayd
againe: *Not doubting but you also of your*
part will assist vs with your prayers, me-
rits, and good workes. All which is a-
gainst the commen Tenet of learned
men diuines; for all do say that this is
only proper to Christ our head & Me-
diator, who by his paines and passion
did merit grace and glorie for others,
be cause the grace which he had (from
whence all the valour of true merit
proceeded) was giuen vnto him not as
he was a priuat man only, but as he
was the head of the vniuersall Church
as St. Thom. 3. p. q. 19. art. 4. proueth
out of the holy Scriptures: how then
can Religious Superiours make their
subiects merits auaileable to others,
seeing it is certaine, that the increase of
grace which euerie good worke doth
merit, togeather with the proportion
of

of glorie and reward in heauen, correſ-
ponde ſo aboundantly to the meaſure
& valour of the worke, that no mere
is due vnto it, either for him in whom
it is, or for any other. Therefore Religious Superiors in this point ſeeme
to take vpõ them more then any Saint
hath arrogated vn to himſelfe, of what
degree ſoeuer he was.

3.   To this I anſweare that Religious
Superiors are neither ſo ignorant nor
ſo arrogãt as by ſome they weare made
to be: for although in the words aboue
cited they ſpeake iointly of *grace and
merits*, yet are they to be vnderſtood
according to the natures of the workes they ſpeake of : ſo that when they
do apply to thier benefactorsthe future
ſatisfactorie works of their ſubiects,
they doe it by way of communication
of the valour of ſuch ſatisfactorie
workes as à ſumme of money might
be deuided amonghſt them; the nature
of ſatisfaction being ſuch, that if it be
rightlie applyed, it may auaile an other
man as much as it would benefit him
by whom it is made, according to the
                              common

common receiued opinion of diuines.
Nauar de Indulgentijs not.31. num.18.
Graffius in appendice lib.2. cap.2. n.
18.19. & 21. Nugnus in Additionibus
q.25. numer.11.quæstiuncula 2. versu
Tandem notandum. pag. 452. & art.3.
diff.1. versu Ad nouum argumentum,
& q.26. art.1. con.6. Corduba lib.5. de
Indulgentijs q.42. versu Qartum dictum pag. 489. versu 8. Dictum. Sotus
in 4. dist. 21. q.1.art.4. sub finem. Sua-
rez in 3. p. tom.4. disp.48. sect.8. num.
26.& disp.55. sect.5. nu. 3. and manie o-
thers cited by them.

4. And when Religious Superiors
speake of application of the valour of
their subiects meritorious workes, either passed or to come, it is by way of
obsecration, or beseeching of allmightie God, vnder this title to bestow his
blessings & graces vpon their friends;
as St. Cyprian did in his first Epistle
vnto Cornelius, *Vt in meritis, & laudi-
bus vestris, nos quoque participes ac socios
computemus* : That we also may acounte
our selues participant and copartners of

C   *your*

your meritts *and praises.* And St. Augustine in his first booke of epistles. epist. 37. *Vt qui bonis meis meritis me video valde indigere, vestris me possem aliquantulum per charitatis communionem miscere:* That I *who find my selfe to suffer very much, in the pouerty of my owne merits, may by the communion of charitie reape some share in yours:* and againe in the same epistle : *Peto etiam vt beatitudo vestra me in eandem charitatem suorum meritorum communium aliquatenus dignetur admittere :* I beseech *your pietie that you will vouchsafe to admit me in some degree in to the same charitie of your common merits.*

5.   In like manner St. Francis de Paula in his letters of Confraternitie vsed these words: *Quemlibet vestrum ad Confraternitatem nostram recipio, in vita pariter & in morte plenam & specialem participationem omnium charismatum & operum meritorum &c.* I receiue each one of you into our Confraternitie, admitting you to a full and speciall participation of all graces and meritious works. And so doth

the

the Catholique Church in the ordinarie praiers made to Saints; as for example in the common of Confeſſors: *Eius*
intercedentibus meritis, ab omnibus nos ab-
ſolue peccatis; Abſolue vs frō all our ſinnes,
by the interceſſion of his merits. And in
the cannon of the Maſſe : *Quorum me-*
ritis præcibuſque concedas, vt in omnibus
protectionis ſuæ muniamur auxilio; graūt
by their merits and praiers that we in all oc-
caſions be armed, with the helpe of thy
protection.

6. Laſtly the holy Scripture in ſun-
drie places vſeth the ſame phraſe. Ge-
neſ. 17. *Recordatus Deus Abrahæ libera-*
uit Lot ; God mindfull of Abraham freed
Lot. And 4. Reg. 11. *Propter Dauid ſer-*
uum tuum ; For Dauids ſake thy ſeruant
&c. And Pſalm. 131. Salomon ſaieth:
Memēt o Domine Dauid & omnis manſue-
tudinis eius ; Lord call to mind Dauid and
all his meeknes. Where Bellarmin writeth, that *Deus vult orari per merita iuſ-*
torum ; God will be intreated by the merits
of iuſt men.

7. If all this ſuffice not to cleare this
C 2 point,

point, then reade Corduba, de Indulgentijs quæst. 39. Nauar. Miscel: 11. de Rosario numer. 7. Rodriquez qq. reg. Tom.1. quæst.34. a.5. and in them you will find the schoole distinctiō of Condigne and Congruous merits, of which dependeth the solution of this difficultie. Because there is no doubt at all, but our good works by way of impetratiō (in which they are called Congruous merits) are not only à great helpe towards the sauing of our one soules, but also towards the assistance of others. For whatsoeuer we do, that is pleasing in the sight of God; doth not only purchase à reward for that which is past, but also deserueth, by the way of Congruitye, helpe for the time to come, to witt, that we may perseuer to the end, and go forward in vertue, and withstand our ghostly enimyes, ouercome our passions, suffer that which is hard and difficult; in fine to attayne whatsoeuer may conduce to our saluation.

8.   And this impetration may not only
be

be conferred vpon an other by the will
of him in whom it is, as all diuines do
hold and prooue manifestlie out of holy Scripture, but by the Prelats and Superiors of the parties to whom it apper-
tayneth, either by deligatiõ from the
Pope, or by their ordinarie power and
authoritie; or by the consent of their
subiects, as Cassarubius affirmes in his
compend: of priuiledges, verbo Indulgentia; and Rodriguez in his reg. qq.
To. 1. q. 35. ar. 2. doth relate à priuiledge
graunted by Vrbanus V. to all Generalls of Orders to graunt this communication of good workes. And Sorbo
in his compend. of priuiledges nameth
sundrie Popes who gaue the like to
Generalls of diuers Orders, which priuiledges by meanes of communication
in priuiledges are now made common
to all.

9.   But indeed this needed not, as Roderiquez prooueth manifestlie in the
place euen now cited, and the authority
aboue mentioned in the third chapter
of this treatise num. 3. out of the end of

C 3   the

the Appendix intituled Apostolatus
Benedictinorum in Anglia, sheweth it
by the practise of locall Superiors.
And out of good reason : for if locall
Superiors by the cannon law may by
admitting any one to the habit & profession of their Order, make him à ma-
teriall child of the same; why may they
not also make any one an adoptiue
child of the same Order, by giuing him
the letters of Fraternitie, by the vertue
of which vnion, there followeth, as will
be sayd in the last chapter of this little
treatise, as it were by naturall consequence, an application of the merits &
good workes done in the Order to
which they are vnited, by way of speciall impetration. This is the common
opinion of Doctors; as Rodriquez saith
à boue, where he citeth St. Tho, Sotus,
Corduba, Paludàn, Rich. Nauar, and
others.

10.   And if there weare anie doubt
of this, yet seeing that whosoeuer maketh himselfe à member of any company, family, or societie, hath à virtuall
                                                                    or

or interpretiue will to submit himselfe
to the laws, customes, and ordinances
of the same society ; all that make
themselues religious men of anie Order whatsoeuer; where this custome of
communication of good works is giuen to lay men by their Superiours, do
giue their consent vnto that custome,
to the end their good works, may be
communicated vnto others by way of
impetration or congruous merit, of
which way of communication, no
Catholike can doubt with à safe conscience.

CHAPTER VI.

The third difficultie concerneth the losse,
which Religious subiects may be thought
to suffer by their superiours for-
wardnes in giueing their let-
ters of Fraternity to lay
persons.

1. THE two former obiections (as
appeareth by the answering of
them) weare but mistakes, or rather
miscon-

misconstructions of other mens laudable intentions : but now we are comming to treate of à more reall doubt; for if what hath beene sayd aboue concerning the proper nature of satisfaction be true, and that Religious Superiors haue power to applye the future satisfactiõs of their subiects vnto their speciall deuoted friends, it will follow that the poore subiect, when he hath spent his whole life in great mortifications, may truly say.

Sic vos, non vobis fertis aratt a boues.

As Oxen plow and others reape the gaines.

So God. knows who shall profitt by my paines.

Because his debt in purgatory may be well nigh as great, as if he had donne but the least part of those austerities for the benefit of himselfe alone: which seemeth somwhat hard.

2.   Therfore we propose heere this question : *Whether Religious Superiors, who do giue to their friends letters of Fraternity, do not wrõge theire subiects notablely; or deceiue their benefactors craftelie?*

The

The reaſon whereon this difficulty is grounded, is becauſe they know full well that their ſubiects ſatisfactions are not infinite, and that therefore euerie part and parcell of them, muſt be diminiſhed by manifold diuiſions : as we ſee in an apple; the parts where of, being equally deuided amongſt ten perſons, muſt needs be leſſe, thē the parts of the ſame deuided amongſt fower. And cōſequently the good Religious man we ſpeake of, who by his daylie penances might well haue beene quited from tenne yeares debt in purgatorie, may come to be there for the ſpace of nine of thoſe tenne yeares, in caſe his Superiors doe diſtribute his ſatisfactions equally amongſt nine others beſides himſelfe.

3.   To this I anſwere that Superiors do only beſtowe amongſt their friends the ſuperabundant ſatisfactiōs of their Religious ſubiects, which otherwiſe by naturall conſequence as they are members of the myſticall body of Gods Church, or by the diuine ordinance, would

would be transferred to the common treasure of the Church, to the end they be not lost, as alltogether vnprofitable, as you may read in Peirinus in Relig. Prælato q. 3. c. 6. Nauar; Miscell. 11. de Rosario num. 9. Nugnus in supplem. q. 26. art. 1. Corduba de Indulgen. qu. 39. Rodriquez qq. reg. q. 33. ar. 4. Valentia in controu. l. de Indulg. c. 5.

4.   Out of which it doth not follow that Religious do take vpon them to giue Indulgences, contrarie to the opinion of diuines, who say, that no prelats inferiour to bishops can by their ordinarie power bestowe anie Indulgences on their owne subiects, much lesse on others: for if you please to reade S. Tho. in 4. dist. 20. q. 1. ar. 4. q. 1. Palatius ibidem dist. 20. disp. 4. in fine. Passarellus in notandis priuilegiorum notab. 22. you will find that such participations do differ from Indulgences in very many things.

5.   But now you will obiect vnto me the second part of the proposed difficulty : that the Superiors do deceiue
their

their friends egregiously; bycause now adayes it is hard to find amongst Religious men any such superabundant satisfactions, as in former times were very frequent in Religious Orders.

6. To answere this obiection fully I must intreat the reader to consider that lay people, by being admitted into the Confraternity of any Religious Order, reape wonderfull many benefits (as will be seene hereafter;) but here I will only speake of three, which amongst the rest seeme most general, and comprehend vnder them more particulars. The first is, that by way of impetratiō, obsecration, and congruous merit, they are made in an especiall manner participant of all good workes which euer from the beginning of that Order haue beene or yet are donne in it. Secondly that they may gaine such Indulgences, as by the Sea Apostolique are graunted vnto that Confraternity. Thirdly that by way of distribution and voluntary application they haue à share in all such satisfactory works of penāces, fastings,

wat-

watchings, disciplines, and the like, as
are, and shall be donne by the Religious of that Order during the time of
their life, and after their death, as long
as they shall haue need of them; that
is, as long as they remaine in the mili-
tant or patient Church, vntill they
come to the triumphant, wheare they
will haue no more neede of any such
helps.

7.   Now where as the difficultie
which we now handle in this chapter
is only touching this third benefite of
future satisfactory works not yet applyed to any person, and abstracteth
from all other benefits whatsoeuer,
the prudent reader will easily obserue,
that though it weare true that the satisfactions of Religious persons now
à dayes weare indeede so deficient
as the obiection makes them to be: yea
though Religious Orders weare come
to that ebbe of satisfactory works, that
they should haue more need to receaue
helpe in that kind from those verie
persons who they admit to their Con-
                                   fraternity,

fraternity, then they weare able to giue
any of their superabundãce; yet should
not those lay people loose by the bar-
gaine, or haue any reason to esteeme
themselues deceiued; because that pre-
tended insufficiencie would be aboundantly supplyed, & well recompensed
by à farre greater excesse in the two
former benefits, & particularly in the
first. For as it is most certaine that the
number of Gods elect of euerie Order
increaseth dayly both in heauen and
here on earth; so is it also euident, that
the masse of their merits and force of
their intercessions is made inestimably
greater and greater from time to time.
In so much that in this kind, those who
are now in these later ages admitted
to the sayd Confraternity receaue greater helps & more ample benefits; then
others who in any former age were admitted vnto the same confraternity
heretofore.

8.   But to lay aside the consideration
of all other benefits whatsoeuer, and
to speake precisely of that one which
gaue occasion by the foresayd obie-

D   ction

&cion, to wit of the satisfaction which may in these be hoped to be found in Religious Orders, ouer and aboue that measure which each singular Religious person may need for himselfe. I answere to the foresayd obiection, that in all Religious Orders in all ages, in all nations & prouinces, yea and all cloysters, or almost all, God truly all wayes had & yet hath his hidden Sain&s vnknowne to the eyes of the world, the measure of whose merits and satisfactorious works are knowne only to his diuine wisdome, and vse not for the most part (for true Religious persons hide them as much as they can) to appeare to others, except it please God to reuealethem, which comonly happeneth not during their liues. Out of which it followeth, that it is not possible for mortall men to make any setled or certaine comparison betwixt this and former ages in this kind : or to affirme resolutely that the whole masse of superabundant merits and satisfactions of men liuing in any one Religious Order, are not now as plentifull

full or neare as plentifull; yea (who knowes but God) peraduenture more aboundant then it hath bin hearetofore in former ages.

9. This answere might well serue the turne, to solue the obiections euen in that verie behalfe of preset or future satisfactorious works, in which onely it presseth; yet because there are alwayes some (and the like hath bin in all former ages) who can not frame vnto themselues so reuerend an opinion of Religious Orders in that age, in which they themselues do liue, and whose imperfections they see with their owne eyes (the reason whereof is obuious to any wise man) to giue them also satisfaction. I answere thirdly to the same obiection, that if Religious men do not liue so austerely (for that is the thing which such me looke after cheifly) as their forefathers heretofore haue done, yet seeing that those whome we speake of, may and do dayly gaine very great Indulgences for almost euery small thinge they vndertake by vertue of diuers graces, which

haue

haue bin graunted by the Sea Apostolique to sundry Religious Orders (all
which they enioy) as may be seene in
Hieronymus à Sorbo in his booke intituled *Compendium fratrum Minorum;*
verbo Indulgentiæ quoad fratres. I thinke
that no prudent mã can doubt, but that
à good share of superabũdant satisfactions may yet at this time be found a-
mongst them as well as in former
times, when these Indulgences were
not so frequently graunted, and so amply as now they are.

10.   Moreouer (and this shale be the
fourth solution) let the obiector, with
all the eloquence he can vse, vnderua-
lue the superabundant satisfactions
which are to be found amongst Religious persons now adayes, and make
worldlings beleeue that they are as few
as he himselfe takes them to be; would
it therfore follow that Religious Superiors did disceiue their friends egregiously in graunting the their letters of
Confraternity? Surely no good Christian will presume to say so : for if he do,
of necessity he must maintayne these
                                    things

things following which are ouer scan-
dalous. First that all the meritorious
works of Religious persons (mentioned in the foresayd letters soone after
the beginning) which by Superiors, &
by the consent of the Religious themselues, are particularly applyed by way
of congruous merit vnto their friends
and benefactors, are not to be regar-
ded. Secondly that all the graces and
Indulgences which by the sea of Rome
are graunted to Religious, and by the
same authority extended to those who
weare their scapular (spoaken of in the
foresayd letters) as Sorbo sheweth, *verbo, Indulgentia quoad saculares;* and *verbo, Communicatio priuilegiorum* in diuerse
places, are not worth hauing. Of which
two points I haue sayd somwhat a-
boue in the first solution of this same
obiection. And thirdly that disciplines,
fastings, prayings , and other acts
of mortifications, which by Superiors
are ofentimes imposed vpon their Religious, precisely for the benefit of their
benefactors are to be slighted as of no
esteeme: this is an error which can not

D 3   be

be maintayned by any Catholique.
Read S. Thom. opus. 19. cap. 7. S. Chri-
soft. hom. 42. S. Ambr. l. 2. de Abraha-
mo. St. Hierome vpon the 5. chapter
of Hieromie. Gen. 18. 19. 30. numer. 16.
Sap. 18. Ezech: 22. and you shall see
the wonderfull things which God hath
done for others by the merits of good
men.

11.　　Therefore to conclude this answere, I remit you to Aragon. 22. qu.
85. art. 3. §. *quarto est aduertendum*. Corduba lib. 1. q. 3. §. *Si quæratur*. Paludan.
in 4. dist. 45. q. 2. art. 2. to see the benefits and commodities which benefactors do reape by the merits of those
Religious to whose confraternity they
are admitted. This I hope will suffice
for the difficulty proposed in this chapter, neuertheles I shall explicate this
same matter some what more fully and
clearely in the next.

CHAP.

CHAPTER VII.

Contayening a fourth difficultie about the difference betwixt communion of Saincts, and communion of good works, by way of confraternity.

1. BEfore I ended the discourse, it came to my mind that some would be verie desirous to know, whether the benefits which benefactors of Religious Orders do reape by communiõ with them in their good works, (we speake not beare of the benefit of particular Indulgences) be different from those, which belong to all good Catholiques by vertue of the ninth article of the Apostolicall Creede, called *Communion of Saincts* : but I passed it then ouer in silence, because I could not in few words dispatch it, intending to make à new chapter of it; in which I do propose this difficulty; Wheather Religious Superiors by making their friends participant of the good works done by their Religious subiects, do

graunt

graunt vnto them any fauour at all,
which is not common to all other Ca-
tholiks by vertue of the Communion
of Sainéts expreffed in the ninth article
of the Creede.

2.   The reafon of this doubt may be
gathered out of thofe authors writings,
who haue made lardge commentaries
vpon the fayd article ; as alfo vpon the
Canon of the Maffe, and vpon the 118.
Pfal. where it is fayd, *Particeps ego fam*
omnium timentium te : *I am partaker of*
all thofe that feare thee. And laftly
vpon the effeéts of excommunication,
which confifteth in the priuation of
many of the effeéts of Communion of
Sainéts, For out of them may be gathered fo many and fo wonderfull effeéts
of this Communion of Sainéts, that it
will feeme hard to shew how the a-
forefayd benefaétors can reape any
more by communication with Religious men in their good woks , then
others.

3.   But firft I would exhort the reader
to fee what Nauarre in his treatife *De*
oratione, & horis canonicis cap. 20. fayeth

in

in praiſe of the communion of Sainꝑs. Then I would intreat him to read S. Thom. in opuſ. *6*. c. *13*. where he proueth it out of Scripture, and concludeth thus: *Qui in charitate viuit, particeps eſt omnis boni quod fit in toto mundo; Who ſo liueth in charity, is partaker of euery good worke which is done throughout the whole world.* What more can benefaꝑors of Religious men looke for by vertue of their letters of Confraternity?

4. By it the faithfull do not only cōmunicate in externall things, as for example in the diuine office, ſermons, proceſſions (by which they find great increaſe of their deuotions) but by vnion of charitie they become liuely members of à myſticall body, and do communicate with their fellowes in all the fruites of the Sacraments, & diuine ſacrifices, in the diſtribution of the cōmon treaſure of the Church, (that is in Indulgences) in preuenient graces, in ſpirituall comforts, in good inſpiratiōs, and illuſtrations, againſt temptations, which are often giuen for the cōgruous merit of other good people; offered

vp

vp to God for that end, that those,
who now of their owne frailtie weire
like to fall, may get helpe and assistance
from God to withstand their enimy.
In fine they communicate in all, both
internall, and externall good workes
done by others, as in meditationes and
contemplations, in austerities, and in all
other things mentioned soone after the
beginning of the foresayd letters: and
also in the satisfaction of Christ, as it
is applyed in the Masse; for it is proba-
bly maintayned by diuers deuines, that
all good Catholiques (if they be in state
of grace) do receaue some part of remission of the paines due vnto them in
purgatory, for euery Masse which is
sayd throughout the whole world.
This is the opinion of Reginaldus in
praxi fori pæn. l. 29. num. 157. Caietan.
Tom. 2. tract. 3. qu. 2. §. *Qui fit.* Azor.
tom. 1. l. 10. c. 20. & 21. Valq. 3. p. disp.
231. c. 3. & 6. Henriquez l. 9. c. 19. num.
5. Nauar. in manuali. cap. 15. num. 111.
Arag. 22. q. 85. art. 3. §. *Quocirca.* Bona-
cin. *de Sacramentis.* disp. 4. quæst. vlt.
puncto 4. num. 1. & 9. Valentia tom. 4.
disp. 6. qu. 11. p. 1. §. 25. And in fine S.

Thom saith in the place aboue cited,
that *they are partakers of all the good*
works which are done in the vniuersall
wolrd; abstracting from intentions either virtuall or interpretiue, but by naturall consequence, as they are members of the same body in which they
are done. And I pray you what more
can benefactors expect to get by vertue
of their letters of cōfraternity of what
kind soeuer they be?

5. To giue à full answere to this
Wickliffian interrogation , I must
declare the grounds and origin of both
these Communications: which beinge
don , the difficulty will presently be
solued.

6. The mystique body of the Church
consisteth of sundry members vnited in
faith, grace , Sacraments, and in other
things aboue expressed: and is as S. Paul
saith to the Romans cap. 12. to be com-
pared to the naturall body of man,
which is composed of diuers members;
or as S. Iohn saieth 1. Epist. c. 1. v. 3. to
à society or fellowship (wherein all
things are posessed in common.) And
con-

consequently as in à mans body euerie good operation of any one member, is beneficiall to the whole body : soe also in societyes or companies, the gaines of each one redoundeth to the communitý as, *quicquid acquirit Monachus, acquirit Monasterio ; Whatsoeuer any Religious mã gaines, belongs to his Monastery:* so it is in the mystique body of the Church in respect of spirituall goods by vertue of the ninth article of the Apostolicall Creed expressed in these words *The cõmunion.*

7.　Whosoeuer therefore maketh himselfe à member of the sayd body or society, doth according to the nature of them receaue from all the members therof, and also communicate vnto them what may be beneficiall to the whole, & not preiudicious to himselfe by naturall consequence grounded in the vnion and incorporation which he then maketh; or (as some saie) by à virtuall or interpretatiue intention to submit himselfe to the customes obserued in such companies or societies.

8.　Which communication so grounded,

ded, as it is euen now ſayd, either in à
naturall conſequence, or elſe in à virtuall intentiõ, is not made vnto others,
as ſome through ignorance do imagin
by way of diuiſion or diſtribution as
almeſgiuers do deuide à loafe a-
mongſt the poore, alotting to euery
one a part of it : but by way of impetration, or beſeeching of Allmighty
God, that he would be pleaſed to accept of all their good workes, as à mo-
tiue to beſtowe his bleſſings vpon the
worker himſelfe, and vpon all others
that are members of the ſame body, to
the end that his good workes may be
beneficiall to them all; as the naturall
good operations of euery part of à mãs
body, are beneficiall to the whole body
without preiudice to the mẽber which
actually exerciſeth its naturall functiõ.

9.　I ſay without preiudice to themſelues; to ſhew that the valour of our
ſatisfactory works are not thus communicated ordinarily, either by naturall conſequence, or by any generall
intention: for this would redounde to

E　　　the

the preiudice of the party that satis-
fieth, seeing that his satisfactions are
not infinite either intensiuely or exten-
siuely : but they are left to his owne
dispositiō to apply them to others me-
diatly or immediatly; that is, by his Superiours, or by his owne accord:& this
by way of partition or distribution ; as
à summe of money may be deuided a-
mongst all the assotiates of à company
or society, as before hath been sayd and
proued by authority.

10.   This is the true ground of Communion of Saints in the generall mystique body of the whole Church ; by
which the communion and participation of specificall mystique bodyes, to
wit of particular Orders or Congregations, may easily be vnderstood: one
thing being presupposed as à knowne
truth; that the intention of the worker
is all in all in such like applications as
these be; as diuines (who treat of application of the diuine sacrifice, of suffrages, and prayer) doe shew and prooue
efficaciously against some who (not re-
                              flecting

flecting that proportiō is neceſſarily required betwixt the cauſe & the effeɐ,
that it exceede not the vertue of the
cauſe) do hould that good works by
way of impetration are as beneficiall to
euery particular perſon of the commu-
nity, when they are offered to God for
the whole with à general intention, as
when they are preſented vnto him for
this or that indiuiduall man by a peculiar & ſpeciall intention for him alone;
which is directly againſt the doctrine
of S. Tho. in 4. diſt. 45. q. 2. a. 2. qu. 1. S.
Bonau. ibidem com. 3. a. 2. q. 3. Suar. in
3. par. tom. 3. diſp. 79. ſect. 12. towards
the end. And *de virtutibus* tom. 2. l. 1.
c. 27. n. 6. Siluius in 22. q. 83. a. 8. Richar.
in 4. diſp. 45. a. 2. q. 3. Adrian. quodlib.
8. a. 3. Medina in C. *de oratione* cap. *de
valore orationis pro multis fuſæ.* D. An-
toninus in 1. p. l. 10. ca. 1. §. 3. Gabriel *in
Canonem Miſſæ* lect. 17. Nauar. in En-
chir. *de oratione* c. 20. nu. 48. Couar. in
cap. *Alma mater* p. 1. §. 5. num. 9. Azor
Inſtit. moral. par. 1. lib. 9. cap. 33. Comi-
tolius Reſponſ. Mor: lib. 1. q. 42. nu. 13.
E 2   & ſequen.

& sequen. and many more cited by them.

11.   This truth being supposed, I will now answere to the former interrogation; to wit, *what more can Religious mens friends expect from them by vertue of their letters of Confraternity, then all good Catholicks do gett by vertue of the Communion of Sainčts?* If no other benefit weare to be looked for by vertue of those letters ; why did Lewys the french King that liued in time of *S.* Stephen the Cistertian Abbot, of whō *S.* Bernard writeth epist. 45. and Fredericus the Emperour mentioned by Chrisostomus Henriquez in his Menol. p. 240. and Theodoretus an other King of france that ruled in *S.* Maurus his time, cited in his chronicles ad annum 64. Sti. Benedicti, and Tertullus *S.* Placid his Father, of whom Surius writeth in the life of the sayd Sainčt, sue so earnestly for them? Why did *S.* Bennet and all the founders of Religious Orders after him, and à numberles number of learned and sainčtly Superiors

periors

periors where of some hūdreds became
afterwards Bishops, Cardinalls, and
Popes, who haue liued since their time,
deceaue their best friends, by making
them beleeue that they did them à singular fauour by adopting and vniting
them to their Orders by such letters of
Confraternity? Weare there no learned men amongst all the Counsellours
of the sayd Popes, Emperours, Cardinalls, and Bishops? None in any of the
Churches, Prouinces, and Kingdomes
wheare & when this custome florished, that would bid them beware of this
imposture?

12. At least why did none of all the
Commenters vpon holy Scripture
speake of this abuse in all their books,
haueing infinite occasions out of the
text it selfe; as out of the first of Ma-
chab. cap. 12. v. 6. out of the Psalm. 118.
v. 63. St. Paul his Epist. ad Thess. cap. 1.
v. 2. Ad Philipp. c. 1. v. 4. Ad Colloss. c.
1. v. 14. 2. Ad Cor. cap. 8. v. 14. Ad Heb.
cap. 13. v. 16. and out of infinite other
places? Is it possible that all the world
E 3   liued

liued in that ignorance till **Wyckliffe**
càme to preach the contrary peſtilent
doctrine to reuenge himſelfe of the
Monks of Cāterburye for putting him
out of his preſidentshippe? Noe truly.
Seeing therefore that no good Catholique hath euer gone about to do this:
it is euident that ſome thing more may
be expected by the ſayd letters, which
is not ordinarily to be gotten by vertue
of the general communion of Saincts.

13.   And becauſe it is now time to
draw to an end, leaſt that I tranſgres
the command impoſed vpon me; I will
diſcouer this hiddē myſtery, which ſee-
meth obſcure only to thoſe, who are
willfully bent to impugne any thing
which is done for the ſaluatiō of Chri-
ſtian ſoules. Know then that there be
in Religious Orders two ſorts of
people, whereof ſome be natural, o-
thers adoptiue children; yet equal in
moſt things. So that by explicating the
happines & benefits of the one ſort of
children, the benefits of the other are
alſo declared. Therefore I will heare

set downe the happines and benefits which the Religious themselues, who are the naturall children of the Order, do dayly enioye by communication with one an other, according as I find them recited by Hieronimus Platus in the 29. chap. nu. 5. of the first booke of his woorke intituled, *The happinesse of Religious men.*

,, 14. To what a masse (saith he) of
,, infinite treasure must it needs amout,
,, if all the riches of so great an army as
,, allmost all Religious Orders are, be
,, brought into one heape? Prayer,
,, Contemplation, mortification of our
,, passions, strife and victorie ouer ten-
,, tations. An infinite number of good
,, thoughts, some inflamed with chari-
,, ty, some adorned with humility, and
,, other vertues, which all are inter-
,, nall. The punishing of the bodye by
,, fasting, watching, and other austeri-
,, ties, the suffering of diuers incommo-
,, dities, the performing of humble of-
,, fices, paines, labouring for the good
,, of our neighbour, heat and cold,

iour-

„iourneyes to and fro , hazard often-
„times of very life. What can à man
„wish for more , then sitting still (if
„he be so commanded)in his chamber,
„to be partaker of all the labours
„which those of the same Order in so
„many parts and prouinces of the
„world as they are spread do vndergoe
„in preaching & praying, and helping
„of soules; finally in performing de-
„uoutly so many good deeds , or suffe-
„ring patiently , and couragious-
„ly so many euills? Neither can
„any man easily gesse in how many
„occasions the merits of others in Re-
„ligion do afforde vs helpe: for if ten-
„tation rush in vpon vs, they procure
„armour to defend vs: if we be to aske
„any thing of God;or to appeare be-
„fore his infinite maiesty vpon other
„occasions, we shall not need to feare
„to appeare emptye in his sight : be-
„cause we are put in fauour with him
„not only by our good deeds , but by
„the deserts of others; their influence
„into our prayers adding grace and
weight

,, weight vnto them. What need I say
,, more? Our coldnesse, our faults and
,, sinnes are so recompensed one the o-
,, therside, with the good offices of thē
,, with whom we liue; that he is more
,, pleased with their duty, then prouo-
,, ked with our offences. Thus farre
,, Platus concerning the communica-
,, tion of good works amongst the na-
,, turall children of anie Religious
,, Order.

,, Now if please you to read the words,
which are contained in the often mentioned letters of Confraternitie, where
it is sayd of the adoptiue children of
the Order: *we do make you partaker of all*
the graces and merits of the Order, admit-
ting and accepting of you to the number of
our brethren and benefactors, and commu-
nicating vnto you freely and willingly
from our hearts, the participation and en-
ioying of all suffrages, sacrifices and Mas-
ses, prayers and fastings, disciplines and
almesdeeds, studyes, sermons, recollections
and meditations, mortifications and obe-
diences, and all other laborious actions and
passions

passions and good works what socuer, &c.
And to turne back to the 5. chapter to
read what I sayd there of power which
Superiors haue to do this; & to consider
well what is sayd allready, and by and
by shall be sayd in this chapter concerning such vnions, and of the benefits
which come thereof; it will appeare
plainly, that by letters of fraternity,
much more benefit may be hoped for,
then by à generall communication
which all Christians haue by vertue of
cõmuniõ of Saints. The groũd of which
I haue touched aboue, & now will declare it so amply, & by so familiar an example, that à child may vnderstand it.
16.   Who knowes not but that à
man, as he is à member of any kingdome is capable of diuers rights and
commodities, of diuers graces and fauours which are common to all who
are free dennesons of the same kingdome, and only to them? and as he is à
member of any particular sheire or
prouince of the same kingdome, may
enioy the priuileges of that sheire
                              which

which one of an other prouince cannot vse without à speciall leaue? and as
he is à member of such à towne or city
belonging to the same shire and kingdome may enioy such benefits, & commodities as are common to all the Citi-
zens of that towne, and so proper to
them, that an inhabitant of an other
place cannot make vse of them? and
lastly as he is à member of à Society
or Company of people dwelling in
that sayd towne, prouince and kingdome liuing in common or commu-
nity as Religious men vse to liue, may
share alike with the rest of his fellowes, which therfore are called his
copartners in all their gaines and commodities, that any of them do bring
into such à society? Who is so ignorant
that knoweth not this to be true? And
this being presupposed, who is so silly,
that he cannot explicate the manner of
the communication of good works by
it, as well in the vniuersall Church, as
in particular societies or fellowships of
seuerall Religious Orders and Cogre-
gations?

17. **Lett**

17.   Lett vs set before our eyes for an
example S. Anselme, who as he was a
member of the mystique body of the
Church of God, reaped the benefit of
the communion of Saincts; as he was
Archbishop of Canterburye he had a
speciall part of all the Masses which
weare sayd dayly in that Archbisho-
prick, wheare in he was named particularly : as he was a member of the
Chapter of the Metropolitan Church,
he did communicate with his brethren,
who were the Cannós of that Church
and Monks of S. Bennets Order in
which he professed: and as he had made
a particular league with some deuoute
soules, which he himselfe speaketh of
in his 37. Epistle he enioyed very particularly a great part of their good
works and merits: all which togeather
commeth to make a greater heape of
benefits then are communicated to e-
uery Christian, as he is only a member
of the generall body of the vniuersall
Church of Christ. For as the imme-
diate ground of cómunication of good
                              works

works is the bond or tye which is betwixt the members of the same body; so the straighter and firmer this bond is with the generall & specificall bodyes, the larger, fuller, and more ample must the communion of good works needs be, as proceeding partly from a naturall consequence common to all members of the same body, partly from a generall intention by which they are applyed, and partly by a speciall intention of those in whom they be, and in whose power it is to apply them more or lesse.

18   Of which theare can be no doubt to be made, vnles we do doubt of the Catholique faith; it being so defined in the 8. session of the generall Councell of Constans, wherin Wickliffe was condemned for this proposition amongst others : *No greater benefit* (sayd Wickliffe) *is got by the speciall praiers which are applyed by Prelats and Religious to peculiar persons, then by generall prayers;* that is by the prayers which are offered vp to God by Christians

F   for

for the vniuersall mysticall body of the Church. Which so fully answeares the former interrogation so often spoken of, that no good Catholique can reply any more in defence of it.

Therfore for the conclusion of this little treatise (which neuertheles hath proued longer then I meant in the beginning) I exhort all good Catholiques, who dayly labour with diligece for all such things as may conduce to their saluation, to make great esteeme of such letters of fraternity as before haue bine mentioned; seeing that therby they may gaine those large benefits which haue bin aboue recited.

FINIS.